TO … M AND BACK

Simon Kelner is editor of *Night and Day* for *The Mail on Sunday*. He has been a journalist for fifteen years, many of which were spent on the sports desk. This is his first book.

TO JERUSALEM AND BACK

SIMON KELNER

PAN BOOKS

First published 1996 by Macmillan

This edition published 1997 by Pan Books
an imprint of Macmillan General Books
25 Eccleston Place, London SW1W 9NF
and Basingstoke

Associated companies throughout the world

ISBN 0 330 34705 5

1 3 5 7 9 8 6 4 2

A CIP catalogue record for this book is available from the British Library

Typeset by CentraCet Limited, Cambridge
Printed by Mackays of Chatham plc, Chatham, Kent

To my father
and
To anyone who has ever supported Swinton

CONTENTS

FOREWORD

It was supposed to be a time of homely celebration, a centenary year marked by speeches, commemorative dinners, exhibition matches and the issue of a special set of postage stamps. Instead, rugby league chose to remember 1995 by forsaking its past. Few sports have undergone such a dizzying upheaval as rugby league did in its hundredth year. The creation of the Super League was a drama that began in the boardrooms of the world's most powerful media magnates, shifted to the streets of Featherstone and Castleford, and reached its resolution in an Australian courtroom. In the course of this book, I have attempted to keep pace with those monumental changes but at times it has been like chasing Martin Offiah in full flight. It was entirely in keeping with the nature of this project that no sooner had the original manuscript been completed than a court judgement in Australia blocked the plan to establish the Super League down under, thereby throwing the whole strategy for a worldwide structure into confusion. Similarly, days before this revised edition was completed, an appeal court overturned the previous ruling, and a game that had gambled its future was now queuing up again at the pay-out window.

Back in February 1996, exactly a year after Rupert

Murdoch's audacious coup annexed the leading clubs and players in Australia, and six days before the breakaway league was due to kick off, Justice James Burchett ruled in Sydney that the Murdoch scheme was unlawful and prevented it from starting before the next millennium. As might have been expected, this judgement began a round of claim and counter-claim, and the power struggle between Australia's governing body of rugby league and its country's all-powerful media conglomerate became a matter of legal argument that left a legacy of bitterness and recrimination. Murdoch had already invested £50 million in attempting to launch the Super League in Australia, and was not going to take a courtroom defeat on the chin. His legal team constructed a powerful case, and on 4 October 1996 three judges at the Federal Court of Appeal in Canberra set aside all sixty orders made against the rebel league eight months earlier.

It was a stunning reversal that was greeted jubilantly by the British party, who were on tour in Fiji at the time. In Britain, there had been no such need for m'learned friends to become involved – the official body have willingly embraced the Murdoch masterplan – but success of the new European Super League is inextricably bound up with events in Australia. Had Murdoch lost his appeal, he would surely have closed the file on Australian rugby league and turned his attention towards the union game, leaving the European Super League isolated. 'The pressures that European Super League has had to work under have all been lifted,' said Maurice Lindsay, the chief executive of rugby league in Britain, of the appeal verdict. The fight, however, was not yet over, and perhaps never will be. The Australian Rugby League came out of court determined to appeal against the appeal. That a sport which has survived so many vicissitudes in its hundred-year history is now seemingly at the mercy of one man's patronage and the beneficence of Australian judges is a powerful reason for the game's adherents to look nervously to the future.

There are other, more fundamental, reasons to be fearful, and I hope these are conveyed on the following pages. I have represented many contrasting views but one underlying feeling links them all: without exception, those whose opinion I sought have an abiding passion for rugby league. I would like to think myself among their number.

It has been one of the pleasures of writing this book to have encountered so many like souls, who made themselves available to discuss the future of the game and were happy to help with my research. In particular, I would like to thank Maurice Lindsay, the chief executive of the rugby league, for the time he has found for me in his demanding schedule and for his willingness to allow me to trawl through the minutes of council meetings. His predecessor, David Oxley, a born communicator, was also extremely helpful and provided many insights into the governing of the game. Vic Wakeling, the head of Sky Sports, was another whose time could certainly have been better spent than in talking to me, and I am grateful for his help. In attempting to present a wide range of opinions in the game, and in piecing together the events that led to the birth of the Super League, I could not have managed without the assistance of all the club officials whose views are recorded here.

My former colleagues on various desks at the *Independent*, Neil Morton, Ben Clissitt, Chris Maume, Phil Shaw, Neil Levis, Wyn Harness and Sara Kearney, have all given me much encouragement, usually in the form of: 'Have you finished that book yet?' But they, and many others, have been staunch colleagues. As has the *Independent*'s rugby league correspondent, Dave Hadfield, who has assisted with telephone numbers and advice. Paul Wilson of the *Observer* has played a similarly crucial part.

My brother Martin made sure that I was faithful to the facts, particularly where Swinton were concerned, and I would like to pay tribute to my mother, who has suffered along with her family the declining fortunes of our favourite team. But at least she didn't have to go the games.

I couldn't have completed the book without the patience of my editor at Macmillan, George Morley, and the support of my agent, David Godwin. My dear friend Robert Chalmers played an heroic role, advising on syntax, helping to sharpen up the jokes and providing succour over countless greasy spoon lunches.

Finally, my thanks go to Phoebe, for giving light at the end of the tunnel, and, most of all, to Karen, for putting up with the cigarette smoke, for her tea and encouragement and, most of all, for cheerfully accompanying me on countless trips up the M6.

Simon Kelner
October, 1996

PROLOGUE

And was Jerusalem builded here
Among these dark, Satanic Mills?
Jerusalem, 1804

The poet and visionary William Blake never visited the north of England, yet his rage against the industrialization of Britain has become an anthem for a region whose people have consistently suffered in the factories and mills of a new, brutal age. Blake's famous lines offered hope of spiritual fulfilment in a world beyond the roaring furnaces and the clattering looms. Just before the end of the nineteenth century, the oppressed labourers created something that would engage their desire for independence from the bosses, and that would help them forge an identity outside their working environment. It was a creation that owed less to Blake's mystical vision than to the more everyday matter of economic necessity. The sport of rugby league was born of rebellion and has been, for a century, a source of pride for the people of the north. The handling ball game that was originated at Rugby School in 1823 became very popular when it spread to the industrial areas; its intensely physical nature provided a welcome release from the frustrations of working life. Yet while the northerners showed themselves to be adept at the new game, they could not afford to take the time off work to play it. Their demand to be compensated for lost earnings provided the excuse for rugby's upper class ruling body to cut loose the common scruffs of the north and provided the impetus for the formation of rugby league in 1895.

While Wigan v. Wakefield Trinity may not have been Blake's idea of Platonic heaven, the new sport was in its own way an expression of confidence, a rejection of the same tyranny to which the workers were subjected in daily life. Given its origins, it is hardly surprising that rugby league should occupy a considerable place in the social history of the three counties beyond which it has rarely strayed – Lancashire, Yorkshire and Cumberland. No other sport has such a keen sense of its heritage.

I have watched rugby league for all but the first seven years of my life. It was a legacy from my father for which I am eternally grateful. He took me to Swinton and sat me down next to him in the stand. In the succeeding thirty-one years, the sport has given me, in roughly equal proportions, moments of transcendental joy and profound anguish. It has also added a dimension to my life that only those with their own sporting obsession would recognize. We may not become more rounded individuals as a result (probably the opposite is the case), but the identification with a particular cause does provide a sense of purpose. For the follower of rugby league, this is especially true, if only because that sense of being attached to a cause runs deeper. Even those with a myopic interest in their own team can see the wider picture of the game as a whole. I have met many supporters who, while favouring one club, choose to go to the best match in their area on any Sunday and are able to watch the contest with cheerful impartiality. I don't believe this culture exists to the same degree in soccer. As an official of Batley said when asked whether the more long-suffering supporters would countenance the move to a summer season: 'There are a lot of bloodnuts out there who would come to games in winter whether it was their team or not.' In this post-modern world, much of the appeal of rugby league can be seen as quaint and anachronistic, but the sense of identity it gives thousands of people – and I am enthusiastic to be counted as a bloodnut myself – should not to be decried.

Having lived in London for the past fifteen years, I lay myself open to accusations of semi-detached sentimentality; it's all very well to celebrate this rugged landscape and earthy culture if you don't have to suffer the privations that come with the territory. This is no doubt true, and there is probably more romantic tosh talked about rugby league than any other sport. But even if you spend more time in wine bars than workingmen's clubs, the game fosters a passion that, once instilled, is impossible to shake off.

The impetus for this book comes from the dramatic change that the game is to undergo. As rugby league enters its second century, the future offers hope for financial security, and for greater exposure and recognition over a significantly wider area. Rupert Murdoch's £87 million – the price for switching to the summer, creating a 12-club Super League including teams in London and Paris, and signing an exclusive deal with his BSkyB satellite TV channel – is a massive financial injection into a sport whose sums are usually done in pounds, shillings and pence. But there may be another cost that is incalculable. How much of what rugby league has to offer the world comes from the fact that it retains a certain honesty when set beside other more prosperous, but intrinsically more corrupt, sports? Already, in the scramble to take full advantage of the Murdoch millions, there have been lawsuits, arguments and accusations over loyalty bonuses paid to certain players, over the divisions of the money among the clubs, over injustices in the new structure. What was sport's best example of a stakeholder society has shown signs of turning into a free-market economy where only the rich thrive.

In common with all spectator sports, rugby league must adapt to the prevailing social and economic climate. Similarly, it must share in sport's good fortune to have become a prized commodity for television companies. Nevertheless, it is naive in the extreme to expect that the essential nature of the game will be preserved in the new superstructure. As Murdoch himself told an audience in Australia in October 1995: 'We'll make rugby league look like you've never seen it played before.' Ignoring the unfortunate muddle of ideas in this statement, it is clear that respect for a hundred years of tradition is not high on his list of priorities. But there were other warnings in his mission statement. For instance: 'If we've failed in rugby league, we'll move on to the next sport and the next one and maybe we'll come back to rugby league one day soon, or later. We'll see.'

The handsome deal negotiated by Maurice Lindsay, the chief executive of the Rugby League, with Murdoch's News Corporation runs for five years. Many of the fears within the game are focused on what happens at the end of that period. Murdoch's men will make a hard-headed commercial judgement based on the game's performance in promoting the sale of satellite dishes and subscriptions. At that time, they may decide there's a better game in town. In a desperate attempt to haul itself out of the financial mire, rugby league has adopted a bank-the-money-now, worry-later strategy. The danger is that, in the process, the game may have sold a priceless attribute – its integrity.

This may be a form of the flat earth thinking – perhaps, more accurately, flat cap thinking – that was prevalent a hundred years ago when rugby league shook off the amateur shackles. Or in 1922, when many criticized the changing of the sport's name from Northern Union to rugby league. There will always be critics of change, particularly in the more staid sections of society represented heavily in the north of England. But this time it is different. It is more than the name that is changing. Rugby league has, in recent years at least, been one of the more progressive professional sports in Britain. It has been unafraid (sometimes to a fault) to alter its rules in an effort to improve the quality of play. Its central administration has been shaken up to general advantage, and it has shown a willingness to grasp some of the more difficult problems, like standards of refereeing, violence on the pitch and drug abuse. In contrast to rugby union, it has been willing to take a critical look at itself and act accordingly. Underpinning it all has been a desire for self-advancement based on the injustices of the past. 'We have always been left with the crumbs from the rich man's table,' says Maurice Lindsay, with particular reference to the game's treatment by the BBC. Given that the corporation's contract with rugby league was worth £500,000 a season and the sport regularly delivers better viewing figures for club games than rugby union does for internationals, it is easy to comprehend his resentment. Equally, it comes as no surprise that News Corporation should be regarded as the good guys, paying a reasonable price for a valuable property. But caution needs to be exercised in the drive for progress. Murdoch's money may solve the immediate cash crisis, and it may even lift the profile of a game still harshly undervalued, but the rush to rearrange the sport's furniture raises concerns about heirlooms that have been disregarded.

There is a further equation which has yet to be fully worked out, what might be called the owt-for-nowt formula or, in modern parlance: there's no such thing as a free lunch. The more rugby league is paid, the more they will be expected to deliver. While there have been written assurances from News Corporation that, on matters of governance, the sport is in sole control, there is little doubt that the major responsibility for marketing will fall on the TV paymasters. Sky's initial budget for the promotion of Super League is £3.5 million, and clubs will have to fit in with their marketing ethos. As Lindsay told a meeting of the council of clubs in December 1995: 'Rugby league would be expected to change and update its image to make it more attractive to a wider audience.' He added that all Super League clubs would need to make a commitment to pre-match entertainment and local marketing. 'Major ambition needs to be demonstrated.' A laudable sentiment, but what exactly does the updating of its image entail for rugby league? A rash of new, American-style names, for certain: we already have among our number the Bradford Bulls, the Hunslet Hawks, the Oldham Bears, the Carlisle Gladiators, the Leigh Centurions and, most laughably of all, the Halifax Bluesox. More will follow, no doubt, along the same path. A clean break from the past may well be a positive step, but the core support for rugby league – people who have a pride in its traditions and who identify strongly with the game's lifelong fight against injustice – are unlikely to be taken in by such superficiality.

Similarly, the modern sporting phenomenon that is euphemistically called 'pre-match entertainment' may be a well-intentioned attempt to increase the game's family appeal, but there is a clear possibility of striking a grotesquely false note. Rugby league's attempts to play Busby Berkeley in the past have only opened it up to ridicule; there has been something of a loss of dignity in the build-up to the Wembley Cup Final, while some of the exhibitions before matches in the 1995 World Cup were, at best, an embarrassment. The staging of curtain-raiser matches before the main event is a move to be welcomed, but the cavorting of Sky cheerleaders against the backdrop of a cut-price fireworks display is not. A sense of occasion can be fostered without relying on the outrageous hype that Sky have made their trademark in other areas. Apart from anything else, there is the significant expense involved in making a pre-game show look really good; the Wembley frolic can cost around £40,000, a good deal more if Diana Ross is involved. The Super League in Britain opened with a Tina Turner impersonator.

Clearly, the people at the satellite network feel it incumbent on them to do more of a selling job than the other channels, but their overblown presentation – which, in its worst excesses, encourages boxers to think that the stage-managed entrance is the most important and marketable tool of their trade – can be subversive. Rugby league is about substance, not show. The game is thrilling enough in its own right, and Sky's hysterical soundtrack can often detract from their usually high production values. What's more, rugby league followers can distinguish very quickly between what's bullshit and what's bona fide.

If the Super League is truly to compete with the major leisure activities of the summer, the game must be presented – or packaged, as they now say at rugby league headquarters – in a modern, viewer-friendly, spectator-attractive way. But care must be taken in the effort to shake off the hackneyed images of the past, otherwise one prejudice will be replaced by another. Despite what the vocal (and some may say paranoid) rugby league lobby believes, the game generally gets a fair deal from the national media, but you don't need a long memory to remember the days when coverage was scant and treatment was unfair. And you don't have to be paranoid to believe that those who seek to patronize and wound are only lying dormant. The willingness to adopt specious, Americanized marketing tactics that are so obviously at odds with the essentially down-to-earth nature of the sport offers rich potential for mockery.

You may think that this is simply a reactionary's manifesto. What's the problem with letting off a few rockets, getting a few young women to high-kick on the sideline, or paying some ageing rockers to mime to their old hits? But this is the thin end of the wedge. The marketing credo runs so deep among those who now seek to propel our game forward that it begins to permeate the soul and, sooner rather than later, the only pitch that matters is the sales pitch. Significantly, in November 1995, representatives of the Super League clubs in Britain flew to Los Angeles, courtesy of News Corporation, for a three-day marketing and merchandising conference. They were joined there by their counterparts from the Australian organization. The purpose of the meeting was to indoctrinate the British clubs in the ways of the leading American sporting bodies. In other words, a crash course in the hard sell. The rugby league men heard from some of the most prominent figures in American sport, including Jerry Jones, the billionaire owner of the Dallas Cowboys gridiron team. They were addressed by representatives of all the other major league sports in America, as well as some multinational companies. This is light-years away from the sort of expertise that rugby league could traditionally call upon, even if the game had been so disposed, but it is a matter of debate whether this sort of advice has any relevance to fighting for the custom of the paying public in Huddersfield and Workington. (And, whatever grandiose ambitions rugby league now cherishes, that prosaic challenge remains its most important one.) Nevertheless, rugby league officials who had already begun to refer to their sport as a product are now to be heard using the term franchise when discussing new clubs.

The visit to Los Angeles is mentioned in the November 1995 minutes of the sport's council of representatives. Jim Quinn, the voluble chairman of Oldham, suggested that the words rugby league 'should be dropped at some point in the future'. He added that Super League had the right feel-good factor. This became the ersatz title of the game a month before the first matches were played. Rugby league is rarely used in official communications and, at headquarters, they toyed with the idea of answering the telephones with the words 'Super League'. They decided against it, although, comfortingly, they kept the recording of Tina Turner while callers are waiting to be connected. Rugby league has officially been pronounced dead, seventy-four years after Northern Union was laid to rest. Many within the game – whatever you wish to call it – proudly proclaim that things will never be the same again, as if that in itself is reason to look cheerfully towards a new horizon. But, shamelessly, I fear for what the future might bring. I can hardly express the full extent of my distaste for these horrible new appendages – the Bulls, the Bears, the Hawks, the Bluesox, all brazenly plagiarized from American sport. At least in America many of the team names have a relevance, for example the Miami Dolphins or the San Francisco 49ers or the Milwaukee Brewers. But what's the connection between Bradford and Bulls, or Hunslet and Hawks or Oldham and Bears? (Local legend has it that when Bradford were casting around for a new name, and wanted a moniker that had a quintessentially Yorkshire ring about, the most popular suggestion among long-suffering supporters was 'the puddings'.)

Rugby league clubs, above all, should not be distancing themselves – even in such a seemingly trivial way – from their local support. It is a clear example of the sort of crude, crass ploy that is designed to increase the game's appeal yet tends to have the reverse effect on those who have already pledged their allegiance. John Drake, a spokesman for the rugby league supporters' association and the founding editor of the fanzine *The Greatest Game*, hit more than one nail on the head when giving the Super League a guarded welcome. 'If rugby league hadn't cooperated,' he said, 'Murdoch would have done it anyway. He would have bought all our best players and taken them to Australia. At least this way, the British game carries on. Whether it can take its supporters with it is another matter.' Too much emphasis, in all the discussion of the merits of the Super League, has been placed on the sport as a television spectacle. While it fits better into Sky's schedules in the summer months, there has been little time to canvass the views of the fans over the move. It is, Maurice Lindsay readily admits, 'a giant leap into the unknown', but this is another bill that he is happy to settle at some date in the future.

Lindsay has been kind enough to spend a good amount of his time with me during the researching of this book. I have found him approachable and extremely helpful. In many areas, we have identical views and, as unreconstructed rugby league 'bloodnuts' both, most of our differences are based on what we each honestly believe to be the way forward for our sport. It is on the subject of Rupert Murdoch that we diverge most. Lindsay genuinely couldn't understand why I should find it a pernicious aspect of the deal that rugby league has aligned itself with the Murdoch organization. 'His money is saving the game,' Lindsay said. 'There wouldn't be the same fuss if we were being sponsored by ICI, or any other multinational.' I pointed out that Murdoch's tactics in other areas of his business have often been seen as brutal and anti-competitive, and many people in the north of England still remember him batting for the same side as Margaret Thatcher. They will not quickly forget what Thatcher inflicted on them – and nor should they – and they are unlikely to view Murdoch with anything other than suspicion. But the game has new horizons now, way beyond those dots on the map that are joined up by the M62. There is excited talk of clubs in Newcastle, Birmingham and Dublin, and of television viewers in Asia, South Africa and America. Rugby league probably has its greatest opportunity to develop as a truly global sport, but the desire to capture a new audience threatens to become overwhelming. We must be able to hear those who have forged an identity for themselves and their region through the playing and following of the greatest game. In years to come, the ugly satellite dishes stationed on outside walls will be no more welcome an addition to the landscape than the dark, satanic mills were in Blake's day. We can only pray that what those dishes represent does not destroy our own small corner of Jerusalem.

ONE

MORE THAN A GAME

A heritage betrayed, or a brave new world?

'Stars? There are no stars in this game. Just men like me.'
This Sporting Life, 1960

Few people have better articulated one of the basic virtues of the game of rugby league than Frank Machin, the uncompromising hero of David Storey's powerful novel, which remains a definitive document of life in a northern town in the early Sixties. It was turned into one of the seminal movies of the time by Lindsay Anderson, who, against a backdrop of belching factory chimneys, depicted a hard-working, hard-living world where rugby league occupied a central place in people's lives. The factory chimneys may have gone, but the game remains largely the same. Unlike any other, rugby league is a sport inextricably connected to the region that spawned it, reflecting the values and mores of those communities, whether they be the coalmining villages of West Yorkshire or the mill towns of east Lancashire. And Machin's words still ring true more than thirty years later. Rugby league players can earn enough to escape the hardships of those around them, but do not betray the fact that they are products of the same background. Even though the game is hard –

arguably the most demanding contact sport there is – it is not as hard as real life.

Top players in the modern era can acquire the riches customarily conferred on footballers. They may cruise round town in their sponsored BMWs – they may even turn up with a pop singer on their arm – but this is an environment in which vanity does not flourish. Traditionally, the rugby league player works and lives among the people he represents when he is paid to pull on the jersey at the weekend. Even in an era when the trend is towards full-time professionalism, this remains largely the case. Hugh McIlvanney in the *Sunday Times* said that this gave 'a new dimension to the concept of the sportsman as a household name. Rugby league players were in a position to know the households, and whether they had dogs that bit the postman.' And when players have to clock on with, or meet in the street or in the pub, people eager to remind them of their shortcomings, it is difficult to assume the posture of a star.

No other professional sportsmen have such intimate dealings with their public. During the miners' strike of 1984, players who were blacklegs were jeered by their own supporters, while those who seek privileged treatment are firmly rebuffed. An illustrative story is told by Dave Hadfield in his book *XIII Winters*. A well-known Wigan player, attempting to jump a queue at the bar, asked the barmaid irritably: 'Don't you know who I am?' Her response was to announce: 'Hey, lads, there's a bloke here who doesn't know who he is.' Players mix easily with spectators, often knowing them by name, and in the lower reaches, the crowd are sometimes party to verbal exchanges on the field. During a match at Huyton once, I was among a small gathering who heard a discussion between a coach and one of his players. The pitch was a quagmire and the numbers on the players' shirts were obscured by mud. The coach wanted to replace one of his prop forwards but was unsure whether he sported 8 or 10 in order to raise the number board which signifies a substitution. 'Tom,' he shouted, 'what's your number?' 'Eh?' came the reply. 'What's your bloody number?' the coach asked insistently. The penny dropped for the bemused prop forward. 'Leigh 43289,' he responded. Keith Macklin, in the 1967 book, the *Rugby League Game*, says affectionately of players: 'They are not all intellectuals, they are not all morons.'

Intimacy remains one of the great qualities of rugby league. There is a feeling, shared by players, spectators and administrators, of a deep attachment to the sport that goes beyond its basic appeal as a means of earning a living or as a form of entertainment. Its importance stems partly from the siege mentality built by the struggles of the past hundred years, and partly from a genuine belief that this is indeed, to borrow the title of the supporters' association fanzine, *The Greatest Game*. Northerners, it is said, are well-balanced people – they have chips on both shoulders – and in their celebration of the qualities of rugby league, it is true that all the defensiveness of a region that has felt downtrodden and ill-regarded ever since the Industrial Revolution comes into play.

It has not helped that rugby league has often been placed, hurtfully, alongside whippets, cloth caps and brass bands as symbolic of northern culture. Until relatively recently, there has been an insidiously patronizing tone to even the most laudatory coverage of the game by sports columnists and national television. Even those who should know better have found themselves lapsing into pantomime stereotype. Take this florid extract from the flyleaf of a 1969 volume by Eddie Waring called *Rugby League: the Great Ones*: 'It's as North as hotpot and Yorkshire pudding. It's as tough as teak. It's rugby league – a man's game if ever there was one. Someone once said of rugby union, "A game for ruffians played by gentlemen" . . . Gentlemen have played rugby league. Gentlemen still do. But the hard core of rugby league players, with their cauliflower ears, their broken noses, their busted and bruised bones, would far rather be called, to use a three-letter word, MEN.' Fearful that the image of machismo had not been adequately conveyed, the passage continued: 'It's a down-to-earth game played by down-to-earth people. Good people. Solid people. To use that three-letter word again, MEN.'

Even now, after all rugby league has done to enhance its traditional image, there are still those who relax into the cliché as if it were a armchair. Take John Sweeney, himself a northerner, writing in the *Observer* in early 1996. His thesis was how the purchase of rights to matches in the rugby league World Cup had changed the editorial direction of the cable channel Live TV. 'In one stroke,' he wrote, 'Live TV had gone from hip, yoof *Hello!*-style TV to a homage to Eddie Waring, heaving drinking and northern male bastards.' Or, three years earlier, Michael Herd said in the London *Evening Standard*: 'Londoners don't give a toss for the sport. We see rugby league as a game for ape-like creatures watched by gloomy men in cloth caps. And we always will.' Such wild excesses are increasingly rare these days, but the wounds are not easily forgotten.

Resentment over the way their beloved game was often portrayed turned into a more profound bitterness in the north during the years of the Thatcher administration, with the systematic dismantling of the traditional heavy industries and the collapse of coalmining. The two-nation divide was clearly illustrated in the *Observer* in the mid-Eighties, when the cartoonist Trog depicted the sun shining on a champagne-swilling pair of yuppies in the south, while in the north, the rain was falling out of a dark sky on to a stooping middle-aged couple, whose plaintive cry was, 'They've got their prime minister, why can't we have ours?' In this newly created industrial wasteland, rugby league assumed an even greater importance as a means of expression, as a badge of regional identity.

People play and watch rugby league because it is part of

their birthright, and pride in the game manifests itself in various ways. Hooliganism, for example, has rarely been a problem. There were sporadic outbreaks in the Eighties – a visit to Warrington or Widnes tended to be an uncomfortable experience for away supporters, Huyton were forced from their ground by repeated assaults on spectators and property and, most notably, there was serious trouble at a Good Friday Humberside Derby in 1981 – but even the big games have invariably been free of the difficulties that blighted soccer.

In 1982, 44,000 attended the replay of the Challenge Cup Final at Elland Road, Leeds, and there was just one arrest outside the ground for drunk and disorderly behaviour. The only incident I witnessed was when a Hull supporter, decked out in black and white and wearing a striped top hat, tried to pass himself off as the Minister of Sport in order to jump the taxi queue. On the previous night, Leeds United soccer fans had gone on the rampage in West Bromwich. They were of the same social background as those who populated Elland Road, so it was, and still is, valid to ask why. The simple answer is that rugby league is generally self-policed by people who feel themselves an integral part of the game. For instance, during a match at St Helens in 1995, a coin was thrown from the crowd at a linesman and the television pictures clearly showed spectators pointing out the miscreant to the police. Again, this was thrown into sharp relief by the behaviour of England soccer supporters on the same night when they forced the abandonment of a friendly international in Dublin. Similarly, the shouting of racial abuse (still, worryingly, a problem at some grounds) usually provokes a vitriolic response from those nearby. The behaviour of fans at the Wembley Cup Final has often been held up as an example to all. The celebratory, unthreatening atmosphere at Wembley comes from the prevalent attitude that it is a day as much for the sport itself as for the competing teams and is indicative that supporters are aware of a wider interest being served.

And though it may seem an odd thing to say of a sport which always has the potential for mayhem on the field, player discipline is the envy of many other games. Disputing a referee's ruling is summarily punished, haranguing an official in the time-honoured fashion of soccer is unheard of, and opposing players do not, as a standard reaction, raise their hands to claim victory in every close decision. Cheats do not prosper and phoneys do not survive, and while rugby league is played these days for substantial reward, at its core is a respect shared by players and spectators, a respect which comes from the understanding that they have been entrusted with the preservation of their heritage. Hopelessly romantic though it may sound, rugby league is still the people's game, as soccer retreats further from its natural constituency with every £20 seat installed and every hospitality suite that is built.

So there rugby league has stood for a hundred years, like the only son of a poor family, eager to leave home but never quite managing to cut the ties. This restlessness has troubled the game's adherents for decades. Should it be nourished as a well-kept secret in its own backyard? Or, if it's so good, why shouldn't those beyond its boundaries be persuaded of its attractions? This is a dichotomy recognized by those who prosecute the case for any minority interest; they crave recognition from the outside world, but are fearful of the consequences should their privilege be shared with a new and greater public. For rugby league, the choice was starkly presented in the spring of 1995: stick to your roots and die or expand and thrive. This was the gospel according to many leading figures in the game's administration. The economic climate was harsh. Attendance figures, while relatively stable, were not high enough to sustain the spiralling wages of players and, as 'Framing the Future', a report commissioned by the league, explained in unadorned language in 1994, too many clubs were fighting for too few spectators in too small an area. So when Rupert Murdoch arrived brandishing £87 million, his News Corporation took on the appearance of the Seventh Cavalry. Even those opposed to the nature of the deal to create a summer Super League and its exclusive tie-up with satellite television, even those who felt that signing a contract with Murdoch was little short of doing business with Mephistopheles, and even those who wanted to preserve their sport as a little-known cottage industry, could recognize the financial imperative. The money had to be taken. It was a chance to stabilize the finances of a sport that, as Mike Stephenson, Sky Sport's analyst and cheer-leader-in-chief, said at the time 'was going down the gurgler'. But it was not quite as simple as that.

Rugby league's insularity may have been derided by others, but what is the effect when its appeal is diminished in its heartland? What happens when unanswerable economic logic takes over and clubs wither and die, or merge with others, or when an outside interest alters the natural balance of the game based on viewing figures or television markets? There was no contesting the financial wisdom of closing down small coal-mines and concentrating on the development of 'superpits', but that does not alter the fact that many people were poorer as a result. Why shouldn't we rage against an assault on the essential quality of our lives, against the tyranny of the balance sheet? We have been told repeatedly that most senior clubs are on the verge of bankruptcy. This is almost certainly true, but in my thirty years following the game, the only clubs to have disappeared for ever are those which were founded during that period. There seems to be an inexplicable law of sporting gravity which acts to keep alive those who, by rights, should have expired long ago.

It may be because rugby league is woven into the social fabric and exists to enrich spirits rather than line pockets. Clearly, there is a basic financial equation which must be balanced, but increasingly sport is being regarded as an industry. It was significant that within the several thousand words of the 'Framing the Future' document, rugby league was not once referred to as a sport. Indeed, the report states: 'The study was approached with the basic premise that rugby league is the same as any other business or product.' But it does not make sense to adopt hard-headed criteria for a sport which survives only through the sentimental attachment of its followers, most of whom believe that the failure of the outside world to recognize the attributes of the game is simply their loss. Of course more spectators must be persuaded through the turnstiles. And facilities are in desperate need of upgrading; given a choice between spending a few thousand on a new player or building a ladies' lavatory, most club chairmen, under pressure from coaches and spectators, have traditionally gone for the scrum-half every time.

Image is all, we are told, but some of the venues where Super League games will be played are little short of an embarrassment. It is one thing to invite the world to join the party, but quite another when they are being welcomed to Watersheddings, home of Oldham, or Halifax's Thrum Hall, grounds that remain ramshackle two-up, two-downs beside the well-appointed stadiums of modern-day soccer. Trevor Delaney, a league historian, points out in his 1995 book, *The International Grounds of Rugby League*, that 'in revisiting most of the grounds which appeared in the 1991 edition, it is obvious that very little has changed over the past four years. Rather than providing new spectator facilities, the emphasis has continued to be placed on meeting essential safety requirements.' In that period, soccer, with its access to the millions provided by the Football Trust and huge TV and sponsorship deals, has been able to transform its major stadiums, many of which now dominate city skylines like cathedrals for the twenty-first century. Rugby league has not been able to call on such funds, and the £15 million that has been spent on ground improvement in the Nineties has gone almost exclusively on meeting the requirements of the Taylor

Report into crowd safety of 1990. If the emergence of the Super League is to be of enduring benefit to the game, it is essential that a sizeable proportion of the money flowing in should be used on stadium refurbishment and not on a further escalation of players' wages.

Several of the most historic grounds failed to make rugby league's centenary season in 1995 – the bulldozers had moved in at Huddersfield's Fartown, Swinton's Station Road, Rochdale Hornets' Athletic Grounds, Hunslet's Parkside and Hull Kingston Rovers' Craven Park – while others were awaiting a condemned notice. The construction in 1994 of the magnificent, futuristic McAlpine Stadium in Huddersfield, already commended in architectural awards, gave the game a new venue of which to be proud. Huddersfield, who spent their last years at Fartown against the backdrop of decrepit stands and crumbling terraces, took up joint occupation of the new ground with the town's soccer club. The fresh start ushered a rise in playing fortunes, while the stadium became a perfect arena for representative matches. Others were not so well blessed. Hull KR, Swinton and York, for instance, all now have better-appointed homes with tip-up plastic seats, franchised hamburger bars and extensive car parking, but in the process have lost much of their support.

'Framing the Future' was rightly scathing about facilities for supporters, but added the rider that new greenfield sites were not necessarily the answer. The report stated: 'Clubs that have moved from their original home cannot command the same loyalty that was once there from the local community.' As a number pursue ambitious plans to distance themselves from the primitive surroundings of the past, this is an ominous warning. It is further evidence of the paradox that affects rugby league: the parochialism that is a core strength can often be a barrier on the road to progress. Geoffrey Moorhouse, in his 1989 book *At the George*, eloquently explained the simple charms of some of the traditional venues: 'For the most part, the grounds are not obviously the abode of superstardom and glitzy success, big television deals and players strong-arming everyone in sight with their lawyers in tow; and some will see this as a deficiency in our game. But they are companionable places, where you can be easy with your neighbour, and this is a more precious thing.'

The deal with News Corporation raises other problems. Is the sport to be packaged for viewers or spectators? The committed rugby league fan wants to see the representatives of his or her community engaged in what can be one of the most thrilling of spectator sports; there is no craving for what Sky promote as 'top class action beamed live and exclusive to your living room'. The switch to a summer season will bring benefits for those who have suffered on freezing terraces, and the firm pitches will undoubtedly speed up play, but bloody-minded traditionalists – and they make up a fair proportion of the natural supporter base – will need to be persuaded of the attractions. There are undeniable advantages for Sky, whose winter schedules are crammed full of soccer but have a lack of 'properties' in the summer. This, both Sky and rugby league officials say, is little more than a happy conjunction, and the game may well have taken the decision to move to a summer season in any event. Still, the unsettling feeling persists that television is making the decisions, and if a sport as self-assured as soccer is powerless to prevent the fiddling of fixture dates and kick-off times to suit the schedules, what chance does rugby league have of resisting the men who are now paymasters? As with soccer, games will spread over the weekend, with a mixture of Friday night, Saturday night and Sunday afternoon kick-offs. It was a long haul before supporters took to the switch from Saturday to Sunday as the main match day. There will be no such luxury as fans get used to summer matches at a variety of times; the Super League contract runs for five years, and has to be a success by the end of that period.

At the last winter game played at Castleford's Wheldon Road ground, the *Independent* reported on the mood of the crowd. One fan summed it up: 'Now that they're running everything to suit the television, what happens when Murdoch pulls out in five years' time? There might not be anything left.' I asked Vic Wakeling, the head of Sky Sports, what he would be worried about if he were on the other side of the deal. His reply was honest and brutal: 'I would be worried about what happens five years down the road.' Maurice Lindsay, the chief executive of the rugby league, is unfazed. He points out that, at the end of the five-year run, the sport will have had the benefit of £87 million of Murdoch's money and this will enable it to stand on its own two feet for the first time in living memory. Paul Harrison, the league's media manager, gave a firm rendition of the party line. 'You're always going to get the traditionalist who says "Don't touch my club",' he said. 'But the fact is that some of those clubs wouldn't be there if it weren't for the Super League. It was an open secret that some of them owed a lot of money. The Super League has allowed them to put their houses in order. We'd all like to live off nostalgia, wouldn't we?'

Many in the game also hold up the example of how the advent of soccer's Premiership in 1992 on the back of a massive contract with Sky had revived the sport. However, built into that deal was regular exposure to those who did not have satellite dishes; *Match of the Day* is still a regular fixture for the BBC on Saturday night. Rugby league has no such safeguard. The contract for coverage of the Challenge Cup is still held by the BBC, but the competition itself, which leads to the final at Wembley in early May, has an uncertain place in the revised calendar. If it stays in position, it becomes little more than an early season tournament, while if it keeps its place as the climax of the campaign and moves to October, it then becomes bound up with the play-offs between the British and Australian Super League clubs that, law suits permitting, is a *raison d'être* of the new world. The BBC are keen to continue their involvement and rugby league needs constant exposure on terrestrial television if it is to retain its impact. The transference of certain big events to satellite, while bringing in unprecedented sums, has undoubtedly harmed their standing. In golf, for instance, the 1995 Ryder Cup impinged far less on public consciousness simply for the fact that most people did not get to watch it. Rugby league does not attract people in sufficient numbers to be able to take the risk of disappearing from public view. Sky, also, are cognizant of this danger. As their stock-in-trade hype begins, and the dry ice rolls in, and the portentous soundtrack strikes up, the last thing they want their cameras to focus on is deserted terraces. In the haste to take Murdoch's money, some of these difficulties have been skated over. Likewise, there is the problem of launching the Super League in 1996, a year in which the summer sporting programme includes both the Olympic Games and soccer's European Championship in England. Should the Super League fail to take off immediately, there is unlikely to be a second chance. As any marketing man knows, you only get one crack at launching a new brand.

However, in dressing up an old-established game where attitudes are entrenched, the tendency towards cosmetic change serves only to subvert its essential appeal. The changing of club names is a particular case. We already had the Keighley Cougars, a successful transformation only because it was linked to an aggressive campaign to woo the youngsters of the town. And, remarkably, the same strategy worked for one of the most traditional clubs. Hardly had the details of the Super League been inked in than Bradford Northern – one of the most evocative names in the history of the game – became Bradford Bulls. Immediately, it seemed, the fortunes of the club rose; crowds increased, drawn in by imaginative marketing and well-orchestrated pre-match entertainment, while the team itself presented a serious challenge to Wigan and St Helens. At the end of the first summer season, supporters of the Super League pointed to what had been achieved in an unpromising environment at Bradford – a rise of 50 per cent in crowds and a much higher profile for the game among the youngsters of the city. But attendance hikes at Bradford and at St Helens – stylish winners of the first Super League title – obscured worrying trends elsewhere, particularly at the game's two biggest clubs. Wigan, where supporters did not take to the summer, drew an average crowd of 10,538, some 4,000 less than the final winter season, while Leeds, who finished third from bottom of the inaugural league table, also lost 4,000 from their average gate.

The overall average was skewed by the rises at London Broncos, whose previous season had been in Division Two, and at Paris, whose base was nil. Paris, who finished their first Super League season narrowly escaping relegation, recorded a healthy first-season average of a little more than 8,000, but there was a widespread feeling that here – and elsewhere – the attendance figures were massaged. Dave Hadfield, one of the few journalists not prepared to swallow the party line, wrote in the *Independent*: 'When it comes to announced crowds, this season has been a novel experience. After decades of thinking "there's more here than that", I have spent this year thinking precisely the opposite. Some clubs seem to have given the attendance that comes into their heads, or what they think the market will stand. Some have had people laughing out loud. Figures have not so much been massaged as taken into the back room and given all the extras.'

There are other false notes. The league is now populated with Bears, Hawks, Bluesox, Gladiators, Broncos and Centurions. These crass re-inventions will fool nobody. They have a hollow ring, deeply at odds with the particular integrity of the game, and have all the authentic appearance of a youngster from the backstreets of Salford wearing a baseball cap back to front and a Los Angeles Raiders sweatshirt. No matter how they are re-educated, Bradford will still be Northern to most of its supporters. The vacuousness of the exercise was well expressed by Nigel Wood, chief executive of Halifax, who chose to adopt the Bluesox appendage. 'Whatever nickname we came up with offended somebody,' he explained. 'So we went for a nickname that offends everyone equally.'

Rugby league has modernized its image successfully in recent years. The move from the old Chapeltown Road headquarters in a run-down area of Leeds to a smart new home on the outskirts of the city was long overdue; the pre-match entertainment at big games has generally been orchestrated with a modicum of dignity; the shedding of the 'It's a man's game for all the family' slogan to be replaced by a marketing strategy that focused on the intrinsic attractions of the sport itself. It has been a hard-fought battle for recognition, but rugby league is rarely represented these days in a way that links it with cloth caps or pigeon racing. It is hard to imagine players of the past on TV chat shows, and certainly not being deployed to sell smart clothes, but in recent years the high-street fashion store The Gap used the Great Britain captain Ellery Hanley in a series of striking billboard advertisements. So why bother about these phoney Americanized suffixes for clubs that have been around since the turn of the century? Again, Geoffrey Moorhouse, with characteristic prescience, wrote: 'Even when, if, I am in Another Place, I shall not wish to contemplate a bastard game played by men wearing padded knickerbockers, broken up by time-outs and garnished with goose-pimpled cheer-leaders on the touchline between the likes of Wigan Wildcats and Batley Braves. I shall haunt Chapeltown Road through all eternity.'

Moorhouse's reference to illegitimacy has a particular resonance at this time. Ever since the great split of 1895, both codes of rugby have moved along different tracks and have maintained an intransigent opposition, the Corinthian amateurs on one side and the horny-handed professionals on the other. But by 1995, the lines had become blurred, and rugby union found itself unable to resist the march of commercialism any longer. They were forced to jettison the amateur sacrament and sanctioned the payment of players. This also meant that the gangway between league and union could now take two-way traffic. These momentous decisions came, significantly, just weeks after rugby league had signed up with Murdoch, a deal which illustrated that an outside interest with enough money can change a sport's landscape for ever.

These developments opened up the much larger question of a fusion of the two codes. And if any one snapshot could sum up the monumental shifts in the world of rugby during 1995, it was a headline from the *Guardian* newspaper just before the end of the year. It wasn't so much the headline itself, though that in itself was pretty remarkable – 'Hard talking due over TV deal for Wigan v. Bath showdown' – but it was its positioning, at the foot of an inside sports page. Here was news of an historic meeting between the top clubs in their respective codes of rugby being treated as an almost commonplace event, placed on the page below a despatch from the England cricket tour and alongside an ice hockey report. At almost any time in the past century, this would have been front page news, sport's equivalent of the collapse of apartheid or the demolition of the Berlin Wall. But a year that had begun with rugby union and league maintaining the implacable opposition that had been nourished for a century ended with the barriers being dismantled at every step.

Perhaps the first extraordinary illustration of the thawing of the cold war was the fact that London Broncos – who provide rugby league's only foothold in the capital – were allowed to play matches at the Stoop Memorial Ground, home of Harlequins and a ground in the shadow of Twickenham's monolithic new stands. Even in the past decade, rugby league men have been thrown out of union grounds, and union players have been banned for playing amateur rugby league, but now there are positive moves towards ground-sharing – Wigan with Orrell, Salford with Sale, and Leeds with the town's rugby union club. Incredibly, Wigan were invited to take part in the Twickenham Sevens in 1995, and won the tournament, hardly breaking sweat in the process. Some weeks later, they were back at rugby union's stronghold, playing the second of their exhibition games against Bath. Under league rules at Maine Road, Wigan had demolished the rugby union champions but, even though they were beaten at Twickenham, Wigan provided most of the flowing rugby. Several leading league players went on to play union in the winter of 1996. Among them, Wigan's Jason Robinson and Henry Paul soon became great favourites at Bath; Gary Connolly teamed up with Will Carling at Harlequins; Va'aiga Tuigamala turned out for Wasps. In addition, a steady flow of Welshmen who turned professional went back to play the game of their fathers, and in October 1996, the Welsh centre Scott Gibbs made history by becoming the first ex-league man to go back to play union for his country, representing Wales against Italy in Rome. The whole world of rugby had been turned upside down and the thrust propelling both sports into a new era has all the random force of a raging torrent.

Television these days pays the money and sometimes makes the rules but in the end, the people will decide what they want to play and watch. Whatever happens at the top level, there will always be those whose passion for their game will be expressed on the touchline or pitch at Old Millhillians or Featherstone Rovers. Nevertheless, there is a commercial sense in drawing the best from each code together, particularly if it were for a series of exhibition matches under hybrid rules. The prospect of contests between Bath and Wigan is indeed one to put bums on seats and satellite dishes on gable ends. Whether this presages a more serious and lasting connection between the two games will be decided by the law of sporting economics. If both can be sustained as separate, viable entities, then there is no logic in halving the opportunities. On the other hand, why pay for the rights to broadcast two sports when you can cream off the talent and pay for one? One thing is certain: if the Super League fails – and Rupert Murdoch will surely be the arbiter in that debate – the end is nigh for rugby league as we know it.

If the game wants to compete as a global sport, it clearly must seek to expand beyond its existing territory, to places where it does not belong, among people who will not understand its special appeal. Rugby league has not hitherto revealed an ability to flourish outside its homeland. You can take the game out of the north, it seems, but you can't take the north out of the game. Perhaps its inward-looking approach is one of its fatal failings, but in thirty years' experience on the terraces, I have hardly ever heard a fellow supporter rage that they should be taking more notice of the sport in St Albans or St Austell. We have simply revelled in our own happy discovery, secure in the knowledge that our game was so much better than theirs. One of the more harmful effects of the unseemly rush to pocket the Murdoch cash was that the moral superiority we enjoyed in exposing the hypocrisy of rugby union was lost. Soon afterwards, rugby league was exercising its own form of apartheid, refusing to play against Australians who had signed up for the rival organization to Murdoch's. (The fact that this was the official governing body of the sport down under seemed not to matter.)

Meanwhile, league's leaders in Britain defiantly claim that they still control the game's destiny, but already there is gathering evidence of the naivety of that view. Several months before the scheduled start of the Super League, the *Independent* revealed that a leading player's loyalty contract (an agreement that tied him to the Super League) had passed into their hands and it included the clause that no transfer could be agreed without the approval of News Corporation. This may be a well-intentioned idea – it could prevent Wigan, for example, signing up all the best talent and maintaining their damaging stranglehold on the game's prizes, or it may mean that a club could hold on to their star man – but it is understandably being regarded as a worrying development. The substance of the report was rebutted by the league and by Sky, but this calmed fears only up to a point. And it was not only within rugby league that the tremors were felt. Other, more secure, sports recognized that they could also be prey to the advances of a mogul who would seek to control player movement. Howard Wilkinson, the manager of Leeds United soccer club, said: 'It's Citizen Kane gone crazy. Sport has to maintain its independence if it is to preserve its integrity.'

Rugby league may have already sold its integrity. Its number could be up. Maybe it is little more than a glorious anachronism anyway, the wonder of it being that it has lasted for a century. And if, as is the case, most of its thirty-two senior clubs play in grounds less than half full, the argument for preservation is a weak one. But perhaps all sport is anachronistic in this age of isolationism, at a time when we are supposed to get our kicks on the Internet. That doesn't prevent millions each week pursuing their sporting obsessions. And it will never stop me following the rugby league team my father saddled me with.

TWO

MAN AND BOY

Rugby league – my part in its downfall

The last time I saw my father was on match day. It was late one Sunday morning and he was awaiting an operation in Crumpsall Hospital, a depressing institution a few miles north of Manchester. It was precisely the sort of day which earns Manchester its meteorological reputation: a fine, insidious drizzle was falling and the clouds seemed low enough to touch if you stood on a stepladder.

I couldn't, without a little research, tell you exactly what year it was; 1984, or maybe 1985, or was it 1986? (I have always envied those who, in recollection of an important episode in their lives, can instantly name the date. It's not that I glide through life in an existential blur, or that so much has happened to me that I have a bigger catalogue of memories than others, but I have to think carefully about placing major events in the calendar, and even then I am not certain to be correct.) What I do know is this: his death was framed by two Swinton matches, against Widnes at home and Bradford Northern away. With reference to my programme collection, I can now tell you that he died on Wednesday, October 9, 1985.

The previous Sunday, I had travelled from London with my brother, Martin, to visit my father in hospital. That winter saw us both living and working in the capital, and most Sundays we followed the same ritual; breakfast at Bert's, a greasy-spoon café on the Holloway Road, followed by a struggle with the contraflows on the M1. Though it may seem shameful to admit it now, our eagerness to make the trip on that particular day was only partly explained by filial responsibility. Swinton, newly (and, as things turned out, temporarily) promoted to the first division, were at home to Widnes that afternoon and the mixture of trepidation and excitement we felt as we set out on the motorway was, in my case at least, as much to do with seeing Swinton as visiting my father. Anyone who has crossed the line from supporter to fanatic will recognize these guilt-inducing feelings. In my case, it was fairly simple to rationalize them: Dad had introduced us to Swinton before we were old enough to know better, and by the time we did, we were hopelessly smitten. He took great pleasure in the fact that, as a family (or at least the male members of it), we had a deep, common bond. That's not to suggest that the family unit would have crumbled had one of us chosen to support, say, Manchester United, but at least we always had a easy point of contact.

Dad often said that the reason he encouraged us to go to Swinton was that he didn't want to suffer alone, but it clearly went beyond that. This was a legacy in which he could take comfort while he was still alive; we're a blue-blooded family, he would say proudly. (This was a reference to Swinton's colours and not to our lineage.) We were all more than a little obsessive, and the flip side of that particular coin, of course, is that a sense of perspective can be left behind, and matters of life and death appear to take second place to injuries and bad refereeing decisions. So, if he had known what I was feeling as he lay in his hospital bed and I sat behind the steering wheel, he could hardly have had cause for complaint. He wouldn't have wanted it any other way.

My father was not, in the normal course of events, a man

who bore personal discomfort with excessive fortitude, and the illness that had rendered him increasingly immobile had taken a toll on his wry, self-deprecating humour. But he was in good form when we arrived at the hospital, cheeking the nurses, telling us how he had persuaded the sister to telephone in his horse-racing bets, and explaining that he had invented a form of charades that involved miming the names of well-known soups. We performed them all: minestrone, mulligatawny, Scotch broth, green pea. Then, inevitably, our bedside manner took the form of discussing Swinton's prospects. The signs of anxiety that Dad betrayed were, it's safe to say, directed towards his impending operation rather than that afternoon's visit of Widnes, but he was sufficiently exercised to take a keen interest in whether Danny Wilson (a prodigiously talented stand-off and Swinton's only class player at that time) had recovered from a knee injury.

After an hour or so, we disappeared into the dank north Manchester day. The grimness of the surroundings, the gloom of the day and dad's underlying weakness of spirit had not unnaturally plunged us into melancholy. The thought occurred, independently as I later discovered, that we were indeed saying goodbye to him. By kick-off time, such feelings were subjugated. There are few advantages in being a Swinton supporter, but at least you get to retreat into another world for eighty minutes, away from the pressures and insecurities of what may be called real life. There was my father dying in hospital, and here was I experiencing unrestrained joy in Swinton's rickety stand.

Widnes, one of the League's top teams and perennial visitors to Wembley at that time, were far stronger than Swinton, whose own decline over the previous two decades had mirrored my father's. Yet Danny Wilson, playing, as it transpired, his last significant game for Swinton, beat Widnes virtually on his own, scoring one try, making another, inspiring those around him and even finding time to taunt the opposition, a speciality of his when things were going well. The score (and I can remember this without recourse to the records) was 17–6. Hardly a drubbing, it has to be admitted, but one of the most satisfying encounters I can remember. Or maybe its significance comes from its place in the story of my life.

The following Wednesday – the day when my father's operation was scheduled – I rang the hospital for news. Despite my persistent questioning, all they would say was that he was in a critical condition and that they were trying, without success, to locate my mother. This, clearly, was hospital code for the worst. I was encouraged by my colleagues on the *Observer* sports desk to leave immediately for Manchester. I rang my brother and arranged to meet him at Euston. We had several gin and tonics on the journey up and withdrew, as you do in such circumstances, into our parallel universe, reliving Sunday's game, recalling great matches of the past, focusing on the two fixed points of our lives: Dad and Swinton. We were both aware – although we did not express it – that this was the probably last time we could talk about the old man in the present tense. The reality struck at Manchester Piccadilly, where my brother's wife met us at the barrier and didn't varnish the truth. 'He's dead,' she said, bleakly. Dad had not survived the operation.

In the succeeding days, there were many sad duties to be discharged, but none had the choking resonance of having to return to Crumpsall Hospital to collect my father's belongings. There was a small, brown holdall in which were a few clothes, his watch, a purse full of 10p pieces (doubtless for the sister to phone in his cross doubles and yankees) and a letter from my brother. The envelope had already been opened and I took out the contents, three sheets torn from a shorthand pad. The text was an exhaustive account of Sunday's victory, conveying the full drama of the contest, containing more than a note of triumphalism and – unusually where Swinton are concerned – sounding an optimistic note for the future. I noticed that the back of the envelope had been franked by a hospital stamp-pad. It read: 'Received, Wednesday, October 9'. So it was safe to assume that Dad must have read the letter that morning. I have often wondered what he must have felt as he was being wheeled into the theatre, but I am fairly certain that, as he pondered my brother's letter, the heart which was soon to give up must have swelled with pride. Following Swinton for more than half a century had caused my father much anguish and frustration, but at the last, they had come through. He died believing the world wasn't such a bad place.

I was neither born nor raised in Swinton; my attachment to this middling-sized town seven miles north of Manchester runs much deeper than that. Even now, I often say that I come from Swinton, although the truth is that I was brought up in nearby Prestwich, a comfortable but soulless middle-class suburb to the north of Manchester. At least Swinton is on the map, although most people outside the north would know of it only through the eponymous insurance company. I haven't met many people who hear the name Swinton and say: 'Yes, I know, home of the rugby league club who had their best days in the Sixties but have fallen on hard times since. Didn't Ken Gowers play for them?'

On the face of it, Swinton is an unexceptional town on the road between Manchester and Chorley and, with a population of 30,000, it is the second biggest of the five Swintons in England. Theories regarding its origins are split. The most popular view is that it dates back to the 1700s as 'Swinetown' – the place where pigs were kept. However, an alternative hypothesis attributes its name to the Danish king Sweyne, who at an earlier time used the area as a vantage point and resting place when rampaging through the north-west. Either way, its identity has been lost down the centuries. Today it is neither a suburb of Manchester, nor is it a Lancashire town with a distinct character. Rather it has been swallowed up by the urban sprawl that extends towards Bolton and includes other communities of indistinct boundaries like Pendlebury, Tyldsley, Walkden and Farnworth. Swinton has one major crossroads, from which, if you turn through 360 degrees, you can see most of the buildings that matter in the town. Right at the junction is the Bull's Head, a Tetley house. Opposite is a two-storey shopping centre that is a haphazard collection of outlets such as Poundstretcher, Select Seconds, Quality Save, a pawnbroker's and, curiously, three travel agents. Linked to the shops by a concrete stairway is a banqueting centre – The Lancastrian Hall – that was opened in 1970 and is testament to the limited architectural ambitions of that period. That faces the town's most impressive structure, a classic Thirties civic centre which won a national architecture medal in 1938 and which used to be Swinton Town Hall but is now the administrative centre of the City of Salford. Finally, you come to the Parish Church of St Peter.

If you walk 200 yards north from the crossroads, up Station Road, past on one side a club called Rollers (this was once the Wishing Well nightclub – 'We have clubland's best pint,' it boasted in the Sixties) and the ubiquitous DIY superstore on the other. Beyond the railway station, now a stop on the branch route between Manchester and Wigan, you arrive at the spot where, until 1992, you would have found a rugby league ground where once 43,000 were housed, where Great Britain used to play Test matches, where Cup Semi-Finals were staged, and where I fell for rugby league and, more especially, Swinton. No trace remains of this particular field of dreams. The floodlights which were visible for miles around have gone. There is no sign of the tallest, most elegant posts in rugby league. The stands have been demolished, and the terraces broken up to be replaced by a haphazard collection of mock-Tudor three-bedroom starter homes. A visitor to the town would have no idea that there used to be a rugby ground on this site.

One winter's Sunday afternoon in 1995, I took a desultory walk along this route. It was the day of a match, but Swinton now play at a ground six miles away. The only traffic queues on Station Road were for the B & Q car park, and the only people on the streets were carrying shopping from the Tesco superstore. The development on the acreage once occupied by stands and terraces is called Lowry Park ('because the painter came from the area,' I was told), while the different types of houses and the streets are all named, bizarrely, after Welsh places (Milford, Denbigh, Harlech, etc.). I had fantasized that I could walk down Gerrem-on-side Close, or Ken Gowers Avenue, or at least something that paid tribute to the former eminence of this segment of real estate. But no. It was as if it had been the site of a horrible atrocity; all trace had been expunged. I asked the woman in the sales office what had been here before the housing development. 'I'm not sure,' she answered. 'I think it was a football ground.' A football ground? Even making allowances for my partisan opinion, Station Road was one of the most impressive stadiums of rugby league. It was built in 1929 as a fitting memorial to Swinton's achievement of winning all four major trophies in the previous season – they remain one of only three clubs to have completed that feat. Their ground reflected the standing and ambition of Swinton. The proximity to Manchester gave the flavour of a big city club and the stadium, constructed on grand lines, had little of the homely appeal of other venues. It was dominated by an impressive main stand, behind which ran the railway line. Opposite, a grandstand, with a steep terrace in front, ran the length of the field. At one end was an open standing area, at the top of which stood the scoreboard, while at the other end was a covered standing enclosure. The terraces were mainly concrete, but substantial areas were a mixture of shale and earth and, inevitably, were covered with weeds. Up until the late Sixties, when it was always on the rota for representative matches, Cup Finals and the like, Station Road was recognized as one of the top four or five venues in the game. (That the club were justly houseproud could be gauged from the fact that, for a decade, the cover of the programme did not have pictures of the team in action but showed a still-life of the ground. And on the wall of the boardroom hung a magnificent panorama of the stadium taken when it housed its record crowd; 44,621 for a Cup Semi-Final in 1951.)

The state of team and ground followed the same downward curve. Swinton won the League Championship two years in succession in 1962–3 and 1963–4, reached the Challenge Cup Semi-Final in 1965, supplied four players for the Great Britain tour of Australia in 1966, and throughout the decade, had a reputation for inventive, attractive rugby that made them, if not universally feared, then at least respected. In 1969, Swinton beat Leigh 11–2 in the Lancashire Cup Final at Wigan, but this was to prove the last trophy of real significance to reside at Station Road. Even though I had not long previously sat my 11-plus, I remember that crisp October day well. I sat next to my brother and father in Central Park's main stand and was rigid with trepidation and excitement. Swinton scored only one try, by the left winger Mike Philbin, but I didn't see it because everyone in front of me stood up. Alex Murphy, one of the game's great half-backs but a figure loathed by opposition supporters, was playing for Leigh at scrum-half. Against this canny old recidivist was a slight youth called Peter Kenny. Murphy employed all his tricks; he even head-butted Kenny on the blind side of the referee. But Kenny emerged as the hero, kicking four drop goals (this was when they were worth two points, and a try was worth three), including one from the halfway line. I can recall returning home and attempting a solo re-enactment of the game on our back lawn, before going to the newsagent's to await delivery of the Football Pink edition of the *Manchester Evening News*. It was front-page news.

The dip in Swinton's fortunes was visible in many ways. For me, it was registered by where we parked for home matches. Up until my teens, we left home at about 2 o'clock and my father usually squeezed his car into a spot about 400 yards away from the ground. We had to walk across a patch of waste ground, listening on the way to the Tannoy playing distorted versions of Del Shannon or the Searchers, or announcing team changes. Long before my father's final years, we could leave for the match at 2.40 and park almost in the main stand.

Occasional visitors, however, would notice the increasingly neglected state of the stadium. In his 1967 book *The Rugby League Game*, Keith Macklin chose Station Road as one of five rugby league grounds worth highlighting but, even then, he wrote: 'It has an aura of importance only clouded by those worn grandstands and the great mound of banking that would look so much trimmer with concrete terracing and barriers . . . Despite its shortcomings, Swinton is big enough to survive the crisis, and to remain one of the big-match grounds of rugby league.' Sadly, this was not to be. International matches ceased being awarded to Station Road in the early Seventies, but it still hosted semi-finals and Championship finals up until 1984. Even though it had a larger capacity than most venues and was perfectly situated next to the railway and close to the motorway network, making it easily accessible from most towns in Lancashire and Yorkshire, the backdrop of decay was not really suitable for a sport that was making serious efforts to smarten up its image.

An attempt to modernize the ground and enhance its facilities in the Eighties went badly awry. Some leading clubs had used land surrounding or adjoining their ground to build social clubs or small-scale sports centres as a source of extra revenue. Swinton already had a social club, a church-hall-style building close to the ground. The Lions Social Club – Swinton are known as the Lions because when the club was founded in 1867, the players used the Red Lion public house as the changing rooms – opened in September, 1967, and among the early attractions were Tony Kent, 'top comedian from Newcastle-on-Tyne' and 'Ted Ross Entertainments, presenting a shop window show of top line Variety Artistes'. Annual membership was ten shillings for 'gents' and five shillings for ladies and OAPs. But spurred on by the example of neighbouring Salford, whose pioneering move to open a social club behind one of the goal-lines had been a huge success, Swinton's ambition spiralled and they decided to knock down the covered stand at one of the ends and build a squash club. This monolithic structure had all the charm of a prison wall but, more important, the idea itself proved to be less than inspired and it was not long before the squash club ran into financial troubles of its own.

But it took a fire at a football stadium thirty miles away finally to seal the fate of Station Road. The blaze at Bradford City's ground on the final day of the 1985 season which killed fifty-six people had long-lasting repercussions for rugby league. Safety certificates for all sports grounds, which were granted before the start of a season by local authorities and fire officers, were suddenly subject to much tighter conditions. In many cases, particularly for football grounds where large crowds were attracted, this was a sensible and welcome move. Even at rugby league grounds, where attendances were much smaller, the drive towards greater safety for spectators was a positive step. Station Road, with its wooden stands in a state of disrepair, its terraces neglected and crumbling and its narrow exits potential death traps, fell some way short of the new standards. Even though average attendances were fewer than 2,000 in a ground that once had comfortably held more than 40,000, the authorities deemed it unsafe and, at the start of the 1987–8 season with the team just promoted to the first division, the club were told to spend £100,000 on safety measures or the licence would be refused. Eventually, they were granted a certificate, but the capacity was restricted to only 4,000.

Over the succeeding seasons, a similar level of expenditure was required simply to ensure the club were able to open the gates. For Swinton, it quickly became clear that it was to be a struggle every bit as unequal as the one they were having on the field with no money left to spend on strengthening the playing squad. Their only asset – they owned the freehold on Station Road, on the security of which they were able to borrow money from the bank – had turned into their biggest liability. If the ground was on the critical list in the mid-Sixties, it was on a life-support machine by the late Eighties and, with the safety officers pressing and the bank barking, the club had a stark choice: sell the ground and save the club or attempt to soldier on and risk being closed down for good. In terms of the wider world, this was not one of life's great dilemmas. But for the thousand or so remaining Swinton die-hards, the thousands who had given up going to matches because the fare and the facilities were so poor, and for a town for whom rugby league had been a source of pride, it had a deep significance.

For the supporters, it may not have been a ground of which to be proud any longer, but it was our home. (In the sporting lexicon, this word is used advisedly; home ground, home matches, home crowd, etc. In American sport, the word is not used in quite the same way, largely because most spectators do not form a similar long-lasting attachment to their stadiums, while owners do not think twice about moving their club from one city to another.) Teams come and go, coaches are replaced with great regularity, chairmen rise and fall, success and failure is transitory, but a ground is, supposedly, for ever. Not surprisingly, then, supporters have an enduring and profound relationship with their home ground and will proudly declare that they have been sitting in the same seat, or standing with the same mates in the same spot, for decades. Sport – and this is particularly true of rugby league, which has such close ties to its public – demands all forms of loyalty and sentimental attachment for its survival, and you don't have to be dysfunctional to regard being at your chosen team's home ground as comforting as being at, well, home.

When the Swinton board decided, in the height of the summer of 1992, to sell the Station Road ground to a property developer for £900,000 and move in with Bury Football Club, six miles away, it merited only a couple of lines on the Press Association wire service. But to those who cared, it was a blow as grievous as any except for the closure of the club or the changing of its name. I had stood and sat in every part of that ground, drunk in every bar, indeed been drunk in every bar, had watched Swinton beat Wigan in the Challenge Cup, seen them lose to almost everyone at one time or another, been present at reserve team games when the players outnumbered the crowd, danced a conga through the dressing room at a New Year's Eve party and, most importantly, had gone through three ages of man sitting in that main stand (sometimes during the same match). It meant far more to me than any family home I had ever lived in. But at least I was present at the last Swinton game played at Station Road, the traditional Easter Monday Derby fixture against Salford. We didn't know it at the time – the supporters' club notes in the programme issued a cheery 'see you on the terraces next season' – but that 24–16 defeat was to be the final indignity we would suffer at the ground.

The news of the exodus from Station Road took a while to sink in. My father, the most significant sentimental link with Swinton, had gone, and now the place that housed most of my memories of him was about to come under the wrecker's ball.

At least I was able to persuade a friend who lived close to the ground to claim a piece of memorabilia, and he was able to rescue the bench from the stand where we sat for decades and where I, as a child, perched next to my father, mesmerized, listening to him wisecrack with his mates, straining to hear the risqué jokes that were not meant for my ears, and watching him chain-smoke, a man at ease with the world in a manner we rarely saw at home. One by one, his friends stopped going, through a combination of apathy and death, but he nevertheless kept up his stream of often surreal one-liners for anyone who would listen. They were often laced with Yiddish, a language with little currency in Swinton's main stand. And his exhortations were, shall we say, individual. Whereas a high tackle perpetrated by an opposition player would be greeted with cries of 'Send him off' from most of the crowd, my dad would shout: 'Send him back to New Guinea.' (This has been immortalized on a club video, Dad's voice clearly audible above the general indignation.)

In the days following the closure of Station Road, I heard his voice again as a soundtrack to the memories that were spooled back. I remembered the first time I was allowed to smoke a cigarette in front of him – it was before a Cup tie against Bradford Northern when I was sixteen years old; I could hear him chastising the referee, or joshing with the regulars who sat near us. Gallows humour was a prerequisite for anyone involved with Swinton. The club secretary once told me a definitive tale that involved a framed message from the Pope which hung in Swinton's boardroom. The fraternal greeting from the Vatican had been inspired by one of the Pope's cardinals – a man from Swinton – and was hung alongside pictures of great teams of the past. At a board meeting one night, the directors were considering, one by one, a number of transfer requests from some of the club's best players. Just after they had finished this depressing task, a train thundered past and the Papal greeting fell off the wall.

The exasperated chairman leaned back. 'That's all we need,' he said. 'Even the bloody Pope's unsettled.'

Although Dad's health was failing and he found it hard to walk, and Swinton were now among the league's lowest classes, he still made it up the steps into his seat in the stand. In fact, it was sometimes more difficult to get him out of it. During a match against Huddersfield on the last day of the season, an announcement came on the Tannoy that a bomb threat had been made and the stand had to be evacuated (it was one of life's great unexplained mysteries why Station Road should suddenly become a terrorist target). Everyone made their way on to the pitch and, together with the players and officials, milled around. Dad refused to budge. He was a man alone in the stand, defiantly resisting the advice of the stewards, saying that if he moved down to the pitch, he would never get up to the stand again and, in any case, he couldn't think of a better way to go – Swinton were 30 points ahead at the time.

Supporting any team, and especially one like Swinton, breeds fatalism, and Dad often said that he would like to be buried at the cemetery that was halfway between the family home and the ground so that he could be sure that even if we didn't visit his grave, at least we could wave to him on our way to the match. He proved to be one step ahead, because he was actually laid to rest at a site that is on the way from my mother's home to Bury, where Swinton now play. Dad said that, if we cared to, we could chalk the scores on his headstone, but we figure that he probably suffered enough during his lifetime.

My mother plays a peripheral role in the family obsession, although she has an understanding of the depth of feeling. She knows, and fully accepts, that there is usually a dual purpose in our visits to see her, coinciding as they do with Swinton matches. When we return from games, she solicitously enquires after the result and there was a time in the Sixties when she could probably have named half a dozen players. However, to my knowledge, she has only ever been to one match, and that was when my brother's little boy was the mascot. She went home at half-time, unimpressed. She did once come to a match at Keighley, but stayed in the car to finish the *Guardian* crossword, and she joined us on occasional trips to Workington or Whitehaven if it meant stopping off in the Lake District for afternoon tea. Nevertheless, Swinton's vicissitudes of the past two decades have not gone unnoticed by her.

When Swinton first moved to Bury, in the 1992–3 season, I decided to boycott 'home' games, not out of militancy, but to spare myself extra heartache; it was bad enough watching them flail away in the nether regions of the second division at other teams' grounds without having the constant and tangible reminder of lost glories and betrayed hopes. Not that there is anything wrong with Gigg Lane, the home of Bury FC. Simon Inglis, in the *Football Grounds of England and Wales* says it is 'the most attractive in the north-west . . . a most satisfying ground to visit'. There was no gainsaying that it was more comfortable, safer and had much better facilities than Station Road, but that's hardly the point. The plain fact was that it wasn't in Swinton, and we were lodgers in someone else's home. What's more, there was no traditional connection between Swinton and Bury; even though there is relatively little distance between the two towns, there is no direct main road that travels from one to the other, no transport route that takes in both points, and very little exchange of labour.

The club laid on free double-decker buses to ferry supporters, but the move gave many fans a reason to kick the habit. For the final season at Station Road, the average attendance had been 2,702; for the inaugural season at Bury, this had dipped to 1,051. When you are as desperate as Swinton, you ought not to give those who have kept faith down the years an easy way out. It doesn't act as mitigation that the club had no option; the more distance they put between themselves and the community they purport to represent, the harder it is to justify their existence. Not only that, but, as rugby league clubs shamefully followed the example of soccer clubs and changed their strips for commercial reasons, Swinton's classic royal blue with a white chevron was overnight turned into blue and white vertical stripes, a soccer design if ever there was one. It was as if the club were making a point; they were anxious to make a new start, keen to be free of the shackles of the past, and there is nothing necessarily wrong with that. However – and this is where the example of Swinton has a reference to the advent of the Super League – if the future is embraced at the expense of a respect for the past, the very people who are still helplessly committed to the cause will feel a deep sense of betrayal.

The sale of Station Road, and all that went with it, may hardly have registered on the sporting seismograph, but it was a small earthquake in Swinton. It was a further example of the gradual homogenization that many northern towns have suffered in the past two decades. There is no local newspaper in Swinton any longer (the *Swinton and Pendlebury Journal* was first turned into a freesheet and then shut down altogether). Much of its light industry has disappeared to be replaced by prefabricated superstores and cash-and-carry units. Many local shops have given up the unequal fight with the supermarkets. Most of what gave the town a pride in its identity has been lost or eroded. The departure of its rugby league club, and the razing of its stadium, was a massive blow. Protest meetings were held, petitions signed, and a variety of grandiose schemes to bring the club back to the town have been mooted, including one that involved a purpose-built ground as part of a new private prison complex. But as things stand, Swinton retains its rugby club in name only.

My earliest recollection of going to watch Swinton concerns another figure who dominated my young life: Big Chief I-Spy.

In the Sixties, the Chief gave his name to a series of pocket books on various topics that required you to spot objects, for which a sliding scale of points was awarded; for instance, a level crossing might be worth ten points and a country stile would earn you twenty points. Once a book was completed, you could send it off to the Chief himself (c/o the *Daily Express*, I believe) and he would send a badge of honour in return. I must have been six or seven years old and we were on holiday in the Lake District. I had almost completed my *Big Chief I-Spy in The Countryside* volume, with just the odd cowshed or level crossing outstanding, When Dad took me along to watch Swinton play at Whitehaven.

I remember sitting in the small, wooden stand, but how it happened I don't know: my I-Spy book, the culmination of months of exhaustive work, fell down a gap between the rows of seats. Even now, I can recall my sense of distress. I crawled on the floor in an effort to retrieve what was then a lifetime's work. Dad made a token effort to search under the stand, but it was futile. I realize now that it was to be good preparation for the next thirty years; emotional pain went hand in hand with supporting Swinton.

The other thing I brought back from that first game was the programme. I kept it for many years and I came to appreciate that it was a peculiar item. The Whitehaven programme in those days was printed on buff paper, the thickness and consistency of a blotter, and, instead of being stapled in the traditional manner, it was one huge sheet, folded into four, which opened out like a route map. Rather in the way that the design of postage stamps give some clue about the prosperity of a particular country, so this programme, in the way it contrasted with the more glossy efforts produced elsewhere, led me to believe that economic depression was a fact of life on rugby league's north-west frontier. This was an impression confirmed by subsequent trips to Barrow, Workington and Whitehaven. (While on the subject of programmes, Barrow's was, for many years, a thing of beauty. The notes were written by the local answer to James Joyce, his stream of consciousness musings on refereeing decisions, injury problems and club gossip often running to hundreds of words without any punctuation.)

My attachment to Swinton became more intense when I started grammar school in Bury. Almost all the boys supported football clubs, mostly Bury or Bolton but some followed Manchester United or City. I was the only Swinton fan in a school of 600 pupils and, perhaps perversely, I relished the sense of uniqueness. Added to that was the sense of belonging that Swinton gave me, a feeling that has stayed with me since. I didn't live in Bury, so I felt something of an outsider at school, and even though I wasn't a native of Swinton either, I had a badge of identity, something that marked me out and which also gave me some working-class credibility with my rougher schoolmates.

At this point it would have been easy to switch my allegiance to United or City, and I did have a period as a Bury supporter. There were two reasons for this brief flirtation: it helped to cement some friendships at school, and I already possessed a blue-and-white scarf. On one occasion, when fixtures clashed, I chose to watch Bury rather than Swinton, and I doubt that my family would have been more surprised or concerned had I announced that I had enlisted with the Moonies. At eleven years old, watching football – even fourth division Bury – opened up an exciting new world to me. I can remember the thrill of my first soccer game, a floodlit match against Bristol Rovers, and I am sure I left the ground that night thinking this was to be the game for me. That sentiment was no doubt encouraged by the burgeoning adolescent desire for independence, and a feeling that I had discovered this experience on my own and had not been led into it by an accident of birth.

I quickly discovered that what I preferred about football

was the sensation rather than the game. At first, I loved sitting with my mates in the boys' stand close to the corner flag, but then I graduated to the Cemetery End, where the hooligans stood – in the late Sixties, even Bury had its share of delinquents. Not unreasonably, I was excited by the element of danger on the terraces. There was no chanting at Swinton; there was no chasing opposition supporters, and the surge, that frightening tide of bodies cascading down the terraces that was a popular activity at the time, was definitely from an alien culture. All we had at Swinton were three fresh-faced cheer-leaders who entered the arena to the Thunderbirds tune and walked once round the pitch before kick-off. To me, football seemed a much more serious business, and was certainly more attractive for that. Yet while I joined in the ludicrously exaggerated celebrations and surged with the rest of them when Bury scored, it didn't come from the heart. If you find the scoring of a try intrinsically more thrilling than the scoring of a goal, you can never make yourself feel otherwise.

So, although there was a time when my faith in Swinton was tested, it could never fully be shaken. Like an errant husband who realizes that what he had at home was infinitely more fulfilling, my passion was only heightened. Furthermore, Swinton then had a team to stir the senses. With a handful of internationals – including the great Ken Gowers, a slightly-built but seemingly indestructible full-back who could kick goals left-footed from anywhere and who was probably the club's best postwar player (and certainly my father's all-time favourite), Swinton played an open, expansive game that was capable of taking any team apart but, more often than not, collapsed against a side who had a big pack of forwards. However, I was born too late for the championship-winning seasons of 1963 and 1964; how I envy my brother with his tales of how Swinton won their last seventeen games in succession to claim the 1963 title. I have a distinct memory of watching the 1965 Challenge Cup Semi-Final on television, although all I can recall of the match, which Swinton lost 25–10 to Wigan, was us having a try disallowed when the scores were level.

At that time, the holy grail – a first appearance at Wembley Stadium for the Challenge Cup Final – seemed attainable. Swinton have won the Cup on three occasions, and been finalists twice, but their last triumph came in 1928, the year before the fixture was switched to Wembley. They reached the final again in 1932 but, cruelly, this was the only time – apart from the war years – when the match was not held at Wembley.

We all thought 1972 was to be our year. After a routine victory in the first round, we were drawn to play at Leigh, local rivals and holders of the trophy, in the second round. In a match of almost unsustainable tension, Swinton emerged with a 4–3 victory, but only after Leigh had hit the crossbar with a penalty kick minutes from the end. In the quarter-finals, we faced another away tie, this time at Halifax. It was a tough, but eminently winnable, assignment. I clearly remember leaving school the previous Friday afternoon and, as darkness began to fall on a clear evening, my mind was free of all thoughts except for the match. In my own world, the air felt to me to be charged with anticipation. By the Sunday of the game, I was almost in a trance. It was my first visit to Thrum Hall, a ground high above the town of Halifax that is full of character but, on that day at least, seemed less than hospitable.

Nevertheless, it appeared that most of the capacity crowd had come from Swinton, and the roar when the team emerged was tumultuous. Deep into the second half, Swinton, in almost total command, led 8–2. Both tries (these were the days when they were worth three points) were scored by the left winger Don Preston, and the second was the climax of a move that went the length of the field. In the succeeding twenty-odd years, I have rarely experienced such an intense joy as at that moment. I had stood on my seat to see the try being scored; now I was jumping up and down on it, an abandoned expression of what we all believed to be true. Nothing could go wrong now; we were one step away from Wembley.

You can probably guess the rest. With five or so minutes left, Halifax squeezed in by the corner flag to score in the right-hand corner. But it was the conversion, a magnificently struck effort by Bruce Burton, that punctured our confidence. There was now only one point in it. And, with seconds left, Halifax were awarded a penalty – the most dubious of decisions for a Swinton player stealing the ball in a tackle – in centre-field almost on the halfway line. Burton, naturally, kicked the goal and that was that – 9–8 to Halifax.

We have had our fleeting moments since, reaching the semi-final of the John Player Trophy in 1982, on the way beating the hated Salford on their own ground with a try in the final minute; winning the Second Division Championship the following year; gaining promotion in 1986 and going on to win the Second Division Premiership. There have also been odd players (the adjective is used advisedly) worth making the 200-mile trip to watch: Kel Earl, a devastating prop forward who could be as wild as his hairstyle; Green Vigo, the black South African winger who would attempt a lap of honour every time he scored a try; Danny Wilson, a sublime player on his (all-too-rare) day whose enduring legacy is to have fathered the footballer Ryan Giggs; Tommy Frodsham, an audacious stand-off who had a sidestep to die for. The pleasures have been plentiful. But we have never come as close to smelling the hamburgers on Wembley Way as on that Sunday afternoon in Halifax. There have been occasions since when my throat has tightened, but I have always managed to hold back, variously, the tears of frustration, of pride, of joy, or of sorrow. But that was the only time I have shed tears for Swinton.

My father used to say that, if we ever reached the Challenge Cup Final, we would be wheeling him into Wembley in a Bath chair. His own fatalism, as well as Swinton's sharp decline, forced him to revise this opinion; he was sure he wouldn't live to see the day. And as I left Crumpsall Hospital clutching my father's brown overnight bag, the sadness that struck most painfully was that he was proved to be right.

THREE

A BRIEF HISTORY: PART ONE

From 1895 to 1970 – a tale of revolution and decline

All along the feeling has been expressed that freedom from the thraldom of the Southern gentry was the best thing that could happen.

The Wigan Observer, 1895

The sum of 6 shillings will not maintain the loafer who plays for these clubs; to provide football for the real working men will still be the task of the Rugby Union.

Jerome K. Jerome, 1895

These two sentiments – expressed soon after the meeting in the George Hotel in Huddersfield that led to the formation of rugby league as a professional game – clearly identify the depth of the resentment felt at the time between the two codes of rugby. It was a resentment harboured on both sides for the best part of a hundred years and came to symbolize many of the social and economic divisions in England; between north and south, the working classes and the upper classes, the professional and the amateur.

For thirty years or so after William Webb Ellis unsuspectingly invented, in 1823, the handling code of football at

Rugby School, the game was played almost exclusively by the patrician classes of England, men free to pursue their pastimes unencumbered by the tedious necessity of having to earn a living. In the latter part of the nineteenth century, the sport expanded to other areas and, particularly in the newly industrialized north and in South Wales, working men also picked up the ball and ran with it. By the time the Rugby Football Union was founded in 1871, there was already friction between those who thought the game belonged to the privileged few and the artisans for whom sport was a means of physical release from their labours. In the north, where millworkers and miners ('hired roughs', as Jerome K. Jerome called them) made up most teams, the tension was stretched to breaking-point in the final decade of the century.

This was some fifty years before the advent of the five-day week and the manual worker who wished to play rugby on a Saturday could only do so by forfeiting his shift or piece-time payment. Not unreasonably, there was pressure from the players for compensation for their loss of earnings. In 1893, a meeting of the Yorkshire Rugby Union proposed that the rules of this strictly amateur game should be altered to allow players to receive 'broken time' payments for missed shifts. They notified the Rugby Football Union that they would be taking their recommendation to the General Meeting – as it transpired, a serious tactical mistake. It forewarned the game's ruling classes, giving them time to mass their forces against the northern upstarts and, as well as lobbying support for their cause, the authorities made sure they obtained proxy votes from any sympathetic member clubs who could not attend the meeting. An unprecedented number of representatives – 431 – were present at the Westminster Palace Hotel in London on 20 September 1893 to hear Yorkshire's resolution 'that players should be allowed compensation for bona fide loss of time'.

The Yorkshire president, James A. Miller opened the case

by stating: 'The working man has to leave his work and lose his wages to play for the benefit of his club, his county or his country, but he receives no recompense for his loss of wages. Is that fair, right or reasonable?' The debate was long and heated, and the opposition case was based equally on a jealous defence of the amateur ethos and on the patronizing premise that if labourers were paid for playing sport, it would demean them as working men. A total of 120 proxy votes were counted against the Yorkshire proposal – curiously, each individual Oxbridge college was given its own vote – and the final result was a clear victory for the establishment, by 282 to 136. There was much cheering when the result was announced, and despite suggestions that the whole affair had been a fix, it was clear from the mathematics (186 votes were cast by northern clubs) that not even all those representing the north had been of one mind.

That meeting, particularly in the prosecution of the opposing cases which opened up the social and regional conflict that was to rage for a century, was almost as significant as the gathering two years later in Huddersfield. The battle was now joined, and soon afterwards the by-laws of rugby union were rewritten to emphasize adherence to the amateur principle: '. . . only clubs composed entirely of amateurs shall be eligible for membership'. Although the denial of broken-time compensation did not immediately result in any northern clubs resigning from the Rugby Union, the problem was not likely to subside, particularly as the feeling of unjust treatment in the north was only fuelled by accusations of covert payments from the south. For two seasons, the game was held together as one, and Yorkshire continued the dominance of the County Championship that had been established since its inauguration in 1888; up until the split in 1895, Yorkshire had won the title six out of seven times, with only Lancashire interrupting their run in 1891.

Even though the senior clubs in Lancashire and Yorkshire

were pressing for independence from their respective county unions, seeking their own self-governing leagues with payment for broken time, the majority had no wish to cut themselves off from the RFU. However, by the time they gathered at the George Hotel, Huddersfield on the evening of 29 August, 1895, it was clear that the umbilical cord with the game's masters in London would have to be severed. Representatives of twelve Yorkshire clubs and nine from Lancashire sat around the table at the George, and by the end of a long night twenty of them passed the following resolution: 'The clubs here represented decided to form a Northern Rugby Football Union, and pledge themselves to push forward without delay its establishment on the principle of payment for bona fide broken-time only.' The only dissenting voice came from Dewsbury, whose fortunes were on the wane, and who felt they could not compete with the stronger clubs. Runcorn were given the place vacated by Dewsbury, and Stockport, who had sent a telegram to the George in support of the breakaway, were also admitted to the newly formed alliance. The clubs represented at the meeting include many who still form the backbone of rugby league and some who, almost exactly a hundred years later, were invited into the Super League: Batley, Bradford, Brighouse Rangers, Broughton Rangers, Dewsbury, Halifax, Huddersfield, Hull, Hunslet, Leeds, Leigh, Liversedge, Manningham, Oldham, Rochdale Hornets, St Helens, Tyldsley, Wakefield Trinity, Warrington, Widnes and Wigan.

Opinion was divided about the wisdom of the split. While the *Bradford Observer* was unequivocal – 'Of the ultimate success of the new Union there seems to be now very little doubt, except on the part of those who are out and out sticklers for the maintenance of the absolute supremacy of the Yorkshire Union and the Rugby Union itself' – the *Manchester Guardian* had a more measured response, saying that the move was 'likely to have more far-reaching effects than are at present calculated upon'.

The latter judgement has been borne out. The Rugby Union reacted to the northern renegades with understandable defiance, raising the ramparts even higher by stating at their AGM (to loud cheering) that the Northern Union clubs were now to be considered 'professionals' and that 'no club or player might play on the ground of a professional club, and no professional club might play on the ground of a Rugby Union club'. Even though playing standards in rugby union declined without the formidable strength of the northern clubs – England's national team in particular embarked on a run of catastrophic results – there was no doubt that the establishment game shed few tears over losing a body of men for whom, on social grounds, it had always had a distaste. Thus was the estrangement of the two codes confirmed, and we were to wait for a century before there was any softening of this line.

The first fixtures of the new Northern Union took place on the afternoon of Saturday, 7 September 1895. The rules were identical to those of rugby union, with the major exception being that a player would receive a flat-rate payment of six shillings if he could prove that he had suffered a loss of earnings. Momentous though those first games were, they hardly set new standards in entertainment: only ninety-four points were scored in a total of ten matches. Each club played a demanding total of forty-two matches in that opening season, and Manningham finished top of the league, a point ahead of Halifax. The tight, often attritional, style of play in those early days can be deduced from the fact that no fewer than fifty-eight matches finished as draws. As the need to make the game attractive to paying spectators was critical, there was much discussion about how the rules could be adapted to this end. The line-out was widely considered to be the major impediment to open rugby, while there was an experimental 13-a-side fixture played within a month of the inaugural day. But it was not until the start of the 1906–7 season that the major changes were adopted which ensured that it was more than just cultural differences that separated the two codes – 13-a-side was adopted; the line-out was abolished; kicking to touch on the full was penalized; the play-the-ball after a tackle was introduced.

This season also saw the first moves in the game's expansion overseas. During their all-conquering visit to Britain in 1905, the New Zealand Rugby Union tourists – the original All Blacks – had been taken with the Northern Union game, not the least of its attractions being the money available to the players. This became all the greater when some of the squad found, on returning to New Zealand, that they had been sacked from their jobs; others were considerably out of pocket. Their case was taken up by a twenty-four-year-old government official and rugby player from Wellington, Albert Baskerville, who wrote to the secretary of the Northern Union, Joe Platt, to float the idea of a touring party from New Zealand to play under Northern Union rules. He also sent copies of the letter to the clubs themselves. Cloak-and-dagger negotiations culminated in the players leaving the Dominion on 17 August 1907.

They played three games on the way in Sydney – planting the first seeds on what was to be fertile territory for the game – before arriving on British shores aboard the SS *Ortona* on 30 September. They had been christened the All Golds during their stay in Australia – a sarcastic reference to the gold sovereigns that were the currency of their 'professional' ambitions; they played in the same all-black colours made famous by their countrymen two years previously. Included in the party were four members of the 1905 side and an Australian centre-three-quarter, Herbert Harry Messenger (known for ever as 'Dally'), who had joined up with them in

Sydney and later became one of the greatest players ever reared in the Antipodes. Other All Blacks had expressed an interest in joining the voyage but had withdrawn under pressure from the rugby union establishment.

In all, the New Zealanders played thirty-five games in Britain, including an international against Wales and three Test matches with England. The tourists won seven and drew one of their first eight matches, before succumbing to the might of Wigan in front of a crowd of 30,000 (how little changes!). Given that they had had little exposure to, and no experience of, the new rules, it was a splendid start. They were beaten by a late try from Wales, but against the representative Northern Union team they won two of the three Test matches. Even then, the missionary zeal that was to inform many curious decisions made by the rugby league down the years was apparent; the first Test was held at Headingley, Leeds, while the other two were at Stamford Bridge, the home of Chelsea Football Club, and Cheltenham, where only 4,000 turned up.

Nevertheless, the tour was a great success, both financially and in terms of raising the profile of the game. Their playing record, too, showed a modest profit, with nineteen games won and two drawn, Messenger being responsible for 146 points, 101 more than the next highest scorer. They also left a substantial legacy in the shape of the centre Lance Todd, who was signed by Wigan as soon as the Test series was over. Todd, first as a player and then as the uncompromising manager of Salford, became a legendary figure in the British game and the trophy for the man of the match at the Challenge Cup final at Wembley is named in his memory. Meanwhile, Albert Baskerville, whose place in the early history of the game was already secure, never made it back to his homeland. During the return visit to Australia, he was taken ill and died of pneumonia in Brisbane.

Nine days before the All Golds were due to leave for Britain, a secret meeting at Bateman's Hotel in Sydney established the New South Wales Rugby League, and the first clubs in the Sydney area were playing competitively by the turn of the year. The game spread to Newcastle, and then to Queensland, and within nine months, an Australian touring party, with Dally Messenger this time representing the country of his birth, followed in the wake of the All Golds by sailing to Britain. The tour coincided with one by the Australian rugby union team, already known as the Wallabies. It was on this visit that the league men were christened the Kangaroos, and by way of illustration a live kangaroo was borrowed from a zoo and paraded before a match at York. The animal later disappeared in mysterious circumstances. This first tour certainly did nothing to establish the legend of the Kangaroos' invincibility. Of the forty-five games they played, only seventeen were won, and not only were they compared unfavourably with the All Golds, but they were also seen as inferior to the Wallabies, who had a significantly better record on their tour. Worse still, the trip was a financial disaster as a series of industrial strikes in the north had an adverse effect on crowds. The man who had organized the tour, James Giltinan, headed home disconsolately before its conclusion and was later declared bankrupt.

The Kangaroo tourists themselves also returned home a chastened bunch, but the game in Australia was revived by an exceptional entrepreneurial spirit, English-born James Joynton Smith. Hotelier, newspaper magnate and politician, he offered members of the Australian Rugby Union team substantial financial inducements to play a series of games against the Kangaroos under agreed hybrid rules. The average fee for the Wallabies was £100 for three matches, fifty times more than a labourer would earn for his week's work. One by one, the Wallabies signed up and the world's first professional rugby circus (pre-dating David Lord's ill-fated attempt to get a similar exercise off the ground by some eighty years) was launched in front of sizeable crowds, ensuring that Joynton

Smith – later the knighted Mayor of Sydney – recouped his outlay plus a little more. The series turned out to be a four-match affair, with each side winning twice, and had wide-ranging consequences. The Wallabies had professionalized themselves and were therefore forced to turn to rugby league, their defection strengthening the fledgling code at the very time when it needed a push.

From that point, rugby league became the most popular game in New South Wales and Queensland, a supremacy that has gone largely unchallenged ever since, despite the advances made by the Wallabies in the 1980s, culminating in their Rugby World Cup triumph of 1991. The introduction in the Thirties of slot machines to Australia's rugby league social clubs was a significant moment; the clubs became a focus of the community's social activity, while the massive amount of revenue generated by the gambling ensured that the game in Australia never suffered from the same financial hardship as its cousin in the old country.

Britain first sent a touring party to Australia in 1910. Clubs were asked to nominate players 'who will do honour to the Northern Union both on and off the field'. Two trial matches were played before the final selection was made. Under the leadership of Jim Lomas, the Cumbrian centre whose move from Bramley to Salford was the game's first £100 transfer, the squad of twenty-five sailed from Tilbury aboard the liner *Osterley*. By now, the antipathy between the two rugby codes down under had turned into a struggle for the hearts and minds of Australians. It was announced by the Australian Rugby Union that a tour by the New Zealand All Blacks would be staged concurrently with the league series.

'The rugby war is to the knife,' *The Bulletin*, a Sydney-based newspaper, commented, 'and will only end when one crowd is pushed out of existence.' The public may not have seen matters in such apocalyptic terms, but there was little doubt about which code held more appeal: attendances at the league matches far outstripped the rival attractions. For their first match in Sydney, against New South Wales, the Northern Union tourists attracted a crowd of more than 30,000, while the match between New Zealand's union men and the state on the same day pulled in barely 9,000. A trend was determined; more star players turned to the professional game, the public believed that it produced a far more entertaining spectacle, and the future of rugby league was cemented. The 'war' was as good as over. One of the players, Frank Young, wrote home to that effect: 'The rugby union and the Northern Union are fighting like dogs against each other, but the professional game is all the rage. It doesn't matter who you speak to in Sydney,' he concluded, 'they are all for the Northern game.'

The Englishmen won their first two Test matches against the Kangaroos, by seven points and five points, and with the series decided, the Australians drafted in some Maori reinforcements for the third test, now calling their team Australasia. An exciting 13–13 draw was played out in front of a crowd of 40,000, while the replay only four days later resulted in the hosts defeating a weakened and weary English team 32–15. The tour ended with the Englishmen winning fourteen, and drawing one, of their eighteen games. Moreover, they made a significant profit off the field as well, and as a result a four-year cycle of reciprocal tours between Great Britain (as they were to become for the 1914 series) and Australia was established.

These series proved to be fixed points around which the respective domestic structures were built, and insured against introspection in the development of the game in both hemispheres. Collisions between the two major rugby-league-playing nations have provided many highlights in the history of the sport, from the 'Rorke's Drift' Test in Sydney in 1914

– when Britain emerged with victory despite being down to ten men for the final thirty mintutes – to the unbeatable 1982 Kangaroos, a team that helped change the shape of both codes of rugby, right through to the triumph of the Australians, missing players who had signed up for the Super League, at Wembley Stadium in the World Cup Final of 1995. It is lamentable that the only threat to the continuing prosperity of this historic contest is now from within, the internecine squabbling that followed the acceptance of the Super League structure resulting in a split between the official bodies of Britain and Australia.

Another of the game's great institutions – the Challenge Cup – may also in time be a casualty of the brave new world. At the very least, its place in the calendar (Wembley Stadium, last Saturday in April or first weekend in May) and its significance as the showpiece occasion is far from secure. The origins of the Challenge Cup can be traced back almost twenty years before rugby league decided to go its own way. The Yorkshire clubs established their own knock-out competition in 1877, playing for a trophy known as 'T'Owd Tin Pot', and the format was so successful with paying spectators that it was copied by fellow county unions. Like other developments of the time, it met with more support in the north. It was felt by many establishment figures that this was the thin end of the wedge; even a hundred years later, the sport of rugby union was defiantly resistant to the idea of cup and league competitions.

The knock-out tournaments further strengthened the organization of rugby up north, and the large crowds made ground improvements a necessity and heightened public expectations. It was a natural development, soon after the schism of 1895, that a Challenge Cup competition, involving all the Northern Union clubs, was proposed. Antonio Fattorini, a Bradford jeweller and chairman of the Manningham club, had been one of the pioneers present at that meeting at The George, and he was commissioned to make a trophy that would befit the growing ambitions of the new code.

The silver cup, which cost £60, was first contested in 1897, and was won by Batley, who beat St Helens 10–3 in the final before a crowd 13,492 at Headingley. Batley dominated the early history of the Challenge Cup, retaining the trophy the next season by beating Bradford and triumphing once more three years later over Warrington. Sadly, this was to prove the last major success for Batley, whose name, long before the end of the game's first century, was often mischievously invoked as a byword for the parochial nature of British rugby league. Batley – named after a Saxon farmer, Bata, who founded the West Yorkshire township in the eighth century – does, it has to be admitted, have an irredeemably northern resonance. Geoffrey Moorhouse, in his excellent book *At the George*, when contrasting the exotic nature of rugby league on the coast of Queensland with our own less spectacular landscape, begins his chapter: 'This is a long, long way from Batley.' The unfortunate lampooning of the town and club comes largely from the meandering television commentaries of Eddie Waring. But it was in communities such as Batley (with their exposed hill-top ground most inappropriately called Mount Pleasant) that the roots of rugby league flourished. It is ironic that, had the Super League not come along in 1995, Batley would have been promoted to the First Division, and would have been among the game's top clubs for the first time since the Great Depression.

Notwithstanding the success of the Challenge Cup in generating interest and revenue at the turn of the century, some clubs – even one with such high standing as Batley – encountered serious financial problems. It is interesting to note that there was a significant body of opinion that believed an intercounty 'Super League' was the way forward (clubs took part in their respective county leagues at that time). To counter this move, a divisional structure was set up, but that did not stop one of the founder members, Tyldesley, from going to the wall in 1900, and they were followed in quick succession by Liversedge, Stockport and Manningham.

The history of rugby league is littered with casualties. By 1995, a total of thirty-three clubs had come and gone, victims of financial hardship or foolhardy enterprise. Among the corpses are teams from such diverse areas as Newcastle, Merthyr Tydfil, Coventry, Streatham and Willesden, Maidstone and Nottingham. Many other clubs tried relocation and re-invention in an effort to stay alive. The Manchester-based Broughton Rangers, the first team to win the double of League and Cup in 1902, moved to the south of the city in the Forties and took the name of a nearby amusement park to become Belle Vue Rangers. Sadly, and despite their rich history, they disappeared in 1955. The Prescot Panthers, (né Highfield), perennial strugglers at the foot of the present-day second division, are the distant cousins of Wigan Highfield, who joined the League in 1922. They had one season as London Highfield (playing at White City stadium under floodlights in 1933) and have also been based in various locations including Liverpool and Runcorn. They have now come to rest in St Helens. Even Bradford Northern and Hunslet, two founder clubs with proud traditions, have gone out of business only to rise again soon afterwards.

Long before Rupert Murdoch, rugby league was desperate to conquer virgin territory; there was even a suggestion that, after the ground-breaking tour of Australia in 1910, the party would sail back via America in an attempt to take the new game to the new world. But while in certain cases ambition obscured reality, two of the clubs in the Super League – Sheffield Eagles and London Broncos – were born of the league's often derided expansionist policy in the 1980s. London Broncos began life in 1980 as Fulham, playing at the football club's Craven Cottage stadium. Their early history was marked by exceptional success; the opening day triumph over Wigan was watched by a crowd of almost 10,000, while later that season they drew 15,000 for a Challenge Cup tie against Wakefield Trinity.

It seemed at that time that rugby league's long-held dream of establishing the sport in the capital had finally come to fruition. But Fulham's rugby league men were evicted from Craven Cottage, and moved to the soulless environment of the Crystal Palace National Sports Centre, and the impetus was lost. They have since changed their name twice and have played 'home' matches at a total of ten grounds in the London area. The club was taken over by the Brisbane Broncos in 1994, and, even though they were anchored in the second division and still did not have a settled home, they were given a place in the Super League. 'If we are to be taken seriously as a national sport, we must have a club in London,' said Maurice Lindsay, the rugby league chief executive. It is indicative that, in all the wrangling over the constitution of the Super League, few argued against the inclusion of London.

Sheffield Eagles, meanwhile, won a place purely on merit, having finished in the top eight of the First Division. Under the enlightened management of Gary Hetherington and his wife Kath, who went on to become president of the league, the Eagles have put down serious roots in the city. They established a youth programme that has yielded impressive results, and have built an infrastructure that would seem impervious to shifts of fortune. They, too, have had to survive the trauma of moving home, but within ten years of their entry into the league in 1984, they had won the Second Division Premiership twice, had reached the final of the Yorkshire Cup and had supplied a number of players for the Great Britain side. Sheffield's proximity to the heartland of rugby league, allied to the fact that this is a city where sport occupies an important place, undoubtedly made the task easier, but theirs is a conspicuous success story among so many tales of failure.

It was the desire to break out from the traditional areas that informed the decision, in 1922, to drop the title Northern Union. After the First World War, the game needed to reassert its own identity and seek a wider base; 'northern' rooted it as a purely regional sport while 'union' was seen both as an unnecessary throwback to its origins and as an inappropriate link with the amateur establishment. The impetus for change came from the less hidebound Australians, and at the annual meeting that summer, Northern Union became the Rugby Football League. Rugby league was born, and a major breakthrough in putting the game on a bigger stage was just around the corner.

Wembley Stadium was built in 1923 as part of the Empire Exhibition. The Duke of York, later King George VI, cut the first turf in January, 1922, and building was completed a matter of days before the FA Cup Final of 1923 between Bolton Wanderers and West Ham United. The attendance that day was given as 126,047 but unofficial estimates put the actual figure at more than 150,000. The match was only able to start when officials (including the now legendary figures of a policeman on a white horse) cleared spectators from the pitch. That same year, rugby league's Challenge Cup Final between Leeds and Hull drew 30,000 to Wakefield. Even so, rugby league's own grounds could not accommodate crowds on this scale in comfort and, as the decade wore on, there was a growing demand to find a more suitable and sizeable venue for the climax of the season. At the annual conference in 1928, held in Llandudno, it was proposed that the Challenge Cup Final should be played annually in London. The motion was passed by a small majority, and Wembley Stadium was chosen ahead of Crystal Palace. Opposition came from conservative elements in the game, who believed that the showpiece match should be held within the established boundaries. (This, it should be added, is a view that is still prosecuted in some quarters, and was heard often during the 1995 World Cup, when both contests between England and Australia were staged at Wembley.)

The first Challenge Cup Final at Wembley was between Dewsbury and Wigan. While much has changed in the staging of the match since, one innovation that afternoon has remained part of the ritual: before the game, to the accompaniment of the Welsh Guards, the crowd sang 'Abide with Me'. These days, the build-up to kick-off time is punctured with American-style razzmatazz in the shape of cheer-leaders, rock stars and choreographed dancers but even though the tradition of a community sing-song ('She's a Lassie from Lancashire' and 'On Ilkley Moor Baht 'at' were staple offerings) has long since expired, the singing of H. E. Lyte's emotional if rather morbid hymn remains a comforting link with the past.

Wembley's first Challenge Cup Final was deemed a commercial success, and while the attendance of 41,500 was considerably smaller than for the football equivalent, it was only a few hundred less than the record for a rugby league Cup Final. The match itself was something of a disappointment, Wigan winning a dour struggle 13–2. The *Daily News* reported that 'there were many rugby union enthusiasts present in the crowd . . . I doubt whether they went away converts.' The *Daily Telegraph* was more scathing. 'A great many followers of the amateur rugby code', it reported, 'must have been disappointed in the game as a spectacle . . . rarely was a movement carried through with finish and artistry.' Nevertheless, match commentary was broadcast on the wireless, and the main objective was realized: for the first time, rugby league was brought to the attention of the nation as a whole.

Apart from the Second World War years – and in 1932, when the preferred date for the final was not available – the Challenge Cup Final has been held annually at Wembley, but it is only relatively recently that the match has been a sell-out. The biggest crowd for a Challenge Cup Final was, in fact, for the 1954 replay between Warrington and Halifax held at Odsal Stadium, Bradford. Until it was supplanted (only recently, in the *Guinness Book of Records*) by the suspiciously round-figure attendance of 104,000 for a rugby union international at Murrayfield, the official gate of 102,569 at Odsal that afternoon was a world record crowd for either code of rugby. As with the first FA Cup Final at Wembley, the term 'official' is used advisedly; it is reckoned that many thousands more fought their way into that great old bowl of a stadium. If you believe the stories of almost every rugby league man over the age of fifty, many more were caught in traffic jams as far away as Leeds or Oldham.

Today, Odsal is a much tidier and more spectator-friendly venue, but even though its cliff-like banks of terracing are still in use it is a shadow of its former self. If it had been built when the debate over taking the Cup Final to London was raging, it might even have become the showpiece ground of the north. But in the mid-Thirties, it was still the site for a huge corporation rubbish tip. The land was reclaimed by a far-sighted local authority, and a rugby ground of immense, almost unnatural, proportions was constructed. The cost of upkeep has been a constant drain on the resources of the Bradford club and in the Seventies and Eighties, the ground was a mess. In his book *The Rugby League Game*, written in 1967, Keith Macklin captures Odsal's curious mixture of disrepair and grandeur: 'No matter how many patches of coarse grass and weed you see peeping through the stones and the cinders, there is still something intensely dramatic about that pitch, down there in the valley, with the great artificial slopes rearing up on all sides.'

Odsal is rarely used for representative matches and semi-finals. Rugby league now turns to the major football stadiums of the north like Old Trafford, Manchester, or Elland Road, the home of Leeds United, where the only other Challenge Cup Final replay was held, a match of unforgettable drama in which Hull beat Widnes in 1982. But back in the boom years of the Fifties, when many grounds were unable to cope with the massive crowds drawn to the game, Odsal's capacity gave it a pre-eminent position, which was confirmed when it became the first venue to install floodlights in 1951.

In the postwar years of social change and technological development, rugby league prospered, in common with other spectator sports. Attendances reached an all-time high, and of the twenty-six present-day clubs that existed in that period, eleven posted their record-crowd figure during the Fifties while several others had theirs within a year or two either side of the decade. And in the 1948–9 season, the league's aggregate attendance was almost seven million. (This compares with 1.3 million in 1978–9 and 1.6 million in 1994–5.) The golden era was effectively ushered in by the Challenge Cup Final of 1948 between Wigan and Bradford Northern, which saw two milestones passed: it was the first one attended by the reigning monarch – George VI – and was also televised, albeit only in the London region. It was not until the 1952 final that television coverage was national. Both the BBC and the ITA (as it was then) showed an interest in the game, and a series of televised competitions was introduced, including a eight-team floodlit tournament played at various soccer grounds in London. This brought more revenue into the game, but live coverage led to a predictable decline in attendances.

On the field, too, the game had moved on to a new level. Some of the greatest players ever to put on boots were in their prime in the Fifties. These included Wigan's Billy Boston, the runaway train of a winger who was the first black man to play for Great Britain and who scored more than 500 tries in his career; Joe Egan, also of Wigan and a hooker with remarkable ball-handling skills; Lewis Jones, the Welsh winger for whom Leeds paid a record signing fee of £6,000 in 1952 and who rewarded them with a total of 2,960 points;

Brian Bevan, the Warrington wing with pipe-cleaner legs who broke a host of try-scoring records; Arthur Clues, the formidable Australian second row who joined Leeds after the war; Alan Prescott, the St Helens prop forward who led Great Britain to an astounding victory over Australia in Brisbane in 1958, despite playing all but three minutes of the game with a broken arm. Other men who were to put their stamp on the Sixties and beyond – players like Alex Murphy, Tom van Vollenhoven, Neil Fox and Eric Ashton – also took their first steps to greatness in the Fifties. The immediate postwar period saw the establishment of new clubs – Workington and Whitehaven pushed forward at the league's north-west outpost while Doncaster established the first foothold in South Yorkshire. All three were destined to be more than the fly-by-nights of previous (and succeeding) eras.

Perhaps the most impressive advances of the Fifties, however, were made in France. Rugby league was first taken across the Channel in 1933 when Britain and the touring Australians played an exhibition match in front of a crowd of 5,000 in Paris. The climate was right for the professional game, as relations between France and the rugby union authorities were under severe strain at the time because of accusations of professionalism. One of the most disillusioned figures was Jean Galia, a union player from Toulouse who was present at that match in Paris. Galia, who had won twenty caps for France and was also a champion prize fighter, became the father of French rugby league, or *jeu à treize*. In 1934, he captained a party of seventeen on a short tour of Britain which climaxed with a creditable 32–21 defeat by England, and later that year, ten teams took part in the inaugural French league. Apart from a presence in Paris, all the clubs were based in the south, and most were in the shadow of the Pyrenees. (This is a regional balance that still pertains. It is notable that in Britain, Australia and France rugby league has taken a strong hold in areas with distinct cultural identities; it is difficult to avoid wondering how sporting history would have been rewritten had, for instance, the professional breakaway of 1895 been centred in London, or if Paris had become the heartland of the game in France, or, conversely, the centre in Australia had been Perth.) The most significant game in France since those early days was to be the opening match of the Super League, when Paris St Germain beat Sheffield Eagles in front of a crowd of 17,000.

The sport in France could easily have been finished by the Second World War. The Vichy government, aware that many rugby league players in the south had fought in the Resistance, declared rugby league illegal and confiscated the assets of the young organization. But even this failed to quell the zeal of the French, and they rose to fresh heights after the war, twice winning a triangular tournament involving England and Wales and in 1951 and 1955 remarkably beating the Australians on their home turf in Test series. French enthusiasm for the game also resulted in the inception of the World Cup in 1954 – a four-nation competition which ended with Britain beating France in front of 30,000 in Paris. It is a measure of the international expansion of rugby league that, in the 1995 World Cup, eleven nations took part in the senior tournament, while seven other countries contested an emerging nations competition. Sadly, it also revealed how standards in France have fallen behind the rest of the world; they finished bottom of a group including Wales and Western Samoa. It was hoped that the original Super League structure – with a team in Paris and one in Toulouse – would revive the game in France, but Toulouse were soon scratched from the masterplan and there have been persistent doubts about whether Paris will have sufficient playing strength to meet the challenge from England.

France began their decline in the Sixties, even though they began the decade by drawing a Test series in Australia. By 1965, their fortunes were at a very low ebb. In Britain, the

Sixties were embraced with confidence. Crowds were still rising and Bev Risman, the former Leeds player, noted in a review of the 1961–2 season that it was 'not surprising that attendances soared by 25 per cent, while other sporting organizations held inquests into their remarkable slump in support by the public . . . if future seasons provide half as many talking points, I am sure that the game will continue to expand in Britain and throughout the world.' Risman's prediction was sadly off the mark. In an effort to reduce the number of mismatches – there was one league table, but clubs only played others from their own county – a two-divisional structure was introduced for the 1962–3 season. In a characteristic volte-face, this was abandoned two years later, by which time attendances had fallen below two million for the first time since the war. Unsurprisingly, many clubs began to suffer serious financial problems and had to kept afloat by hand-outs from the league. Equally worryingly, the game itself had become dull, one-dimensional and predictable. There were glorious exceptions, like the memorable 1965 Cup Final when Wigan defeated Hunslet 20–16, but the fact that there was no restriction on ball retention meant that many teams adopted conservative tactics; 'get in front then stick the ball up your jersey,' was a common approach. Crowds dwindled, and the optimistic note struck by Risman in 1962 was replaced by concentrated, and sometimes desperate, efforts to breathe new life into the sport.

In October 1966, as an experiment for the BBC's year-old Floodlit Trophy, the rule by which teams had to surrender possession after four tackles was introduced; two months later, it was adopted for all games. A second significant change came twelve months later, when the league sanctioned playing on Sunday. On 17 December 1967, Bradford played York and Leigh faced Dewsbury, even though the archaic Lord's Day Observance Act meant that they couldn't actually charge through the turnstiles. They skirted round the law by making admission by programme only, charging their usual entrance price for the match-day publication. Although both changes received mixed reactions, they were to prove meaningful steps on the road to a brighter future. For the moment, however, it seemed that there was no arresting the decline. A game that had been born of a revolutionary courage was dying from a lack of visionary leadership. In the Seventies, it got worse. But then the story of modern rugby league began to take shape.

FOUR

A BRIEF HISTORY: PART TWO

Beyond 1970 – the making of modern rugby league

Dark clouds had settled implacably over rugby league by the early Seventies. The decline in playing standards in Britain, the consequent drop in attendance figures, the deepening financial crisis, the unsatisfactory relationship between the game and television – a litany of problems needed to be resolved if the sport was not to disappear from the Pennine landscape.

The sun had shone briefly at the beginning of the decade with the performance of the 1970 Great Britain side in Australia and New Zealand. Led by the St Helens stand-off half, Frank Myler, Britain returned with the best record of any touring party down under: played 24, won 22, drawn 1, lost 1, points scored 653, points conceded 288. The only defeat they suffered was in the First Test in Brisbane, a comprehensive 37–15 loss to the Kangaroos. Undaunted, the Lions (as they were now known) regrouped in remarkable fashion. In the Second Test, they overcame the second-half sending-off of the Leeds centre Syd Hynes (who a year later became the first player to be dismissed in a Wembley Cup Final) to win 28–7. The deciding Test, in front of a crowd of 61,000 at the Sydney Cricket Ground, was a momentous occasion. Now it was the Australians' turn to play with twelve men when the giant prop Artie Beetson – no stranger to scenes of skullduggery – was sent off thirteen minutes from the end for landing a punch on Cliff Watson. Despite Britain outscoring their opponents by five tries to one, the result was in doubt until a glorious try in the last minute by the Hull KR half-back Roger Millward – the most consistent performer and leading points scorer on tour – secured a 21–17 victory and the Ashes for Britain.

Many saw this triumph, which excised the memory of the disappointing 1966 tour, as presaging an era of British dominance in the international arena. It turned out to be a false dawn. The sound financial footing of rugby league in Australia (the slot-machines were still relentlessly whirring away) gave them the resources to raise their game. Money was pumped into a national coaching structure, coaches were encouraged to look to other sports for fresh influences (many turned to American football) and, with the ban on international transfers relaxed, they imported some of the British players who had caused them such discomfort on the 1970 tour – notably the powerful Hull KR second row Phil Lowe and Castleford's loose forward Malcolm Reilly, who became a feared presence in the Australian game before returning to England. From that point, Australia did not take a backward step. They regained the Ashes in 1973 and by the time rugby league entered its second century, they had still not relinquished their grip on them.

The victorious British party of 1970 returned to face an uncertain future. The optimism of the early Sixties had long since been dissipated. Contrast Bev Risman's confident proclamations of 1962 (page 70) with the address of Ronnie Simpson, chairman of the league, eleven years later in his introduction to the *John Player Yearbook*. 'During one's tenure of office,' Simpson began his message, 'one likes to think that changes are effected in the game which are of great benefit. Changes have, of course, occurred in every year of the game's history and many that have been the subject of controversy have later shown themselves to be detrimental rather than beneficial.' This could hardly be mistaken for a rallying cry from an administrator determined to press the case for his beleaguered game; it was more a reflection of the depressed state of a conservative leadership not knowing which way to turn. Simpson's oblique statement may have referred to the decision to revert to the two-division format that had been tried unsuccessfully twice before – for three seasons from 1902 and for two seasons from 1962 – for the forthcoming season. Or he could have been alluding to the modification of the four-tackle rule, which had been extended to six tackles in 1972. (Although the four-tackle rule had been almost universally welcomed as an improvement on the stultifying, possession-is-all game of the Sixties, it led to play having an unsatisfactory staccato rhythm, offering little chance for sides to exert real pressure on their opponents. Six tackles would remedy that.) Despite Simpson's misgivings, there proved to be nothing detrimental about either move. Both were crucial factors in the revival of rugby league's fortunes, although it took some time before their full effect was felt.

A clear picture of the deep and widespread financial problems is presented in that same 1973 yearbook. Here are extracts from their day-by-day diary of the 1972–3 season: 'Hunslet report debts of £16,500 and borrow £10,000 from Rugby League . . . Hull KR report loss of £11,818 . . . Announced that rugby league attendances are generally down by 14.5 per cent this season . . . Doncaster face the biggest cash crisis in their twenty-two-year history . . . Huddersfield launch £10,000 appeal to survive . . . £10,000 of Whitehaven's £30,000 appeal fund raised . . .' There was, however, the odd piece of good news; Salford announced a record profit, Rochdale Hornets reported a 40 per cent increase in attendances, and Wigan were booed off the field by their own supporters after defeat by Whitehaven.

At the end of the season, Hunslet, one of the original George Hotel 21, were forced to leave their famous but now decaying Parkside ground in south Leeds. Deep in debt, the club had no option but to sell their biggest asset to a property developer. Hunslet had taken part in a classic Cup Final only eight years previously, but had gone into serious decline almost immediately afterwards. In fact, from the season after their Wembley appearance until the advent of two divisions, they did not finish in the top half of table and the end of the 1972–3 campaign saw them third from bottom of the league, attracting crowds that could be counted in hundreds.

Homeless and downtrodden, the club gave up the will to live, and it seemed another historic name would be scratched from the roll-call. Old rugby league clubs die hard, however, and Geoff Gunney, a veteran second-row forward capped eleven times by Great Britain and who was the last man to leave the field after the final fixture at Parkside, was instrumental in keeping Hunslet alive. A consortium was put together during the close season, and by the time competition recommenced, New Hunslet was born, taking their place in the inaugural Second Division. They played at the Leeds Greyhound Stadium, close to Leeds United's football ground and within walking distance of the suburb of Hunslet. They gained immediate notoriety by using American football-style 'tuning fork' posts, but their first season brought the new club only seven victories and they finished fourth from bottom of the Second Division. Steady progress saw them win promotion three seasons later. In common with several other teams under the four-up, four-down system, they came straight back down again, only for the same cycle to repeated over the succeeding two years. They reverted to plain old Hunslet for the 1979–80 season and, three years later, moved across the road to share Elland Road, Leeds United's palatial home. If the greyhound stadium, with its glass-fronted restaurants in the grandstands and its peculiar posts, provided a strange backdrop, then watching matches at Elland Road, an arena that could hold 40,000 echoing to the shouts of only a few hundred, was a truly bizarre experience. But Hunslet battled on, and in 1986–7 won the Second Division championship. Again, they were relegated the next season. They moved out of Elland Road in 1994 to share Bramley's McLaren Field ground, in preparation for permanent residence at the new South Leeds Stadium.

Hunslet's peripatetic, insecure existence was an extreme example of the struggles that several lowly clubs endured throughout the Seventies. The downward trend in league attendances was not immediately halted by the advent of two divisions, and in 1974–5 crowd figures reached a nadir when fewer than 800,000 went through the turnstiles. Clear evidence of the moribund state of affairs had been laid before the nation in the previous season. The visiting Australians insisted that one of the three Test matches be held at Wembley, the theory being that it gave expatriate Aussies a chance to support their team while also elevating the game to a grander stage. Only 9,874 turned up at Wembley to see the tourists beaten 21–12 in an excellent match. But the image that stayed with millions of viewers who watched the live coverage on television was of a stadium one-tenth full, of vast unpopulated stands and terraces. The tiny attendance necessitated the opening of just one section of the ground and the eerie atmosphere contributed to the overall impression of an unpopular sport with ideas above its station. As an indication of how far rugby league has travelled in the two decades since, the 1992 match between the two nations at Wembley (which, admittedly, doubled up as a World Cup decider) attracted a sell-out crowd of 73,000.

It was a long, hard road to revival. The metaphor is appropriate, as the construction of one of Britain's most ambitious, expensive and important motorways played a highly significant role in the upturn in fortunes that rugby league was to enjoy in the latter part of the Seventies. On 3 August 1971, a 13.2-mile stretch of the M62 crossing the Pennines was opened, significantly easing the passage between Lancashire and Yorkshire. With the completion of this section, which cost £20 million and necessitated the excavation of 1.3 million cubic yards of rock, the M62 ran unbroken for twenty-eight miles from west of Manchester to Windy Hill near Huddersfield. As the *Observer* reported: 'The supreme feat of engineering that this road represents becomes clear as soon as you are on top of the mountains and the road scales the heights, to avoid fog. The road was blasted out of solid rock, the mountain peat proving so glutinous that it was useless for recycling and had to be removed in lorryloads.'

Thus, for the first time, there was a rapid, all-weather arterial route linking the big industrial centres of Lancashire and West Yorkshire. Of lesser importance, perhaps, it meant that rugby league followers in these areas could pursue their passion without negotiating the old A62, avoiding the inevitable traffic jams in Oldham and Huddersfield and without undertaking the risk of a treacherous, often snowbound, ascent over the Pennines. By July 1975, the full 108-mile length of the M62 between Liverpool and Humberside was complete and, apart from the four Cumbrian clubs and those introduced in expansion areas, all points on the rugby league map were, more or less, joined by England's most impressive motorway. Before the M62 was built, it would take a Wigan supporter, for instance, some two and a half hours to travel to Leeds; by motorway, the journey can be done in less than an hour. In cross-Pennine matches, there was suddenly a substantial away following, and today, on a Sunday afternoon, vivid evidence of the mobility of support is provided by the steady stream of Wallace Arnold coaches going one way on the M62 and Walls of Wigan coaches going in the opposite direction.

Rugby league was about to enter a more confident era. A further injection of new hope came in the form of sponsorship money. For the 1971–2 season, the tobacco company John Player and Sons put up £9,500 for a new knock-out tournament – the Player's No.6 Trophy – to be played in the early part of the season, with the final scheduled before the Challenge Cup got under way. The company had already shown an interest in attaching their product to rugby league, sponsoring a man-of-the-match competition, but this new trophy was a substantial investment in a game that, at the time, was going nowhere. The first final, played at Odsal Stadium in front of 7,975, was won by Halifax, who beat Wakefield Trinity 22–11. By the second season of the competition, the prize fund had risen to £16,500, and everyone got a share; from the first round losers, who got £150 each, to the eventual winners – Leeds – who received £5,000.

It has proved to be one of the most enduring sponsorships in British sport. Now called the Regal Trophy (it was changed in 1989 to help the marketing of another John Player brand), the 1994–5 competition saw a share-out of £410,000 and the final, in which Wigan defeated Warrington, was played before a capacity crowd of almost 20,000 at Huddersfield's McAlpine Stadium. However, it seems as if the end of the line is approaching for this partnership; not only does the advent of Super League, and the change to a summer season, mean that it is almost impossible to accommodate the competition in the fixture list, but the hardening of the government line, added to stringent EU directives, is almost certain to result in a total ban on tobacco sponsorship. This will have serious consequences for rugby league, given that beer and cigarette companies have been the major sources of sponsorship revenue for the past twenty years. In 1978, the Challenge Cup was sponsored for the first time, by State Express cigarettes, and the sport's most prestigious trophy became known as the State Express Challenge Cup. Or rather, it didn't. An editorial comment in the *John Player Yearbook* of five years earlier had wisely said: 'Rugby league welcomes sponsorship, but it is not always easy to apply it to existing competitions. For example, if the Challenge Cup were to be replaced by a sponsor's trophy, rugby league's day at Wembley would still be referred to as "Cup Final day". No one would dream of putting another name to the Cup in everyday conversation or, for that matter, in Press comment.'

State Express was indeed one of the less visible sponsorships, but in the six years until the company ceased trading in Britain, the deal had provided £500,000 for the competing clubs. Another cigarette maker, Gallaher and Co, filled the vacuum and the tournament became known as the Silk Cut Challenge Cup. In 1994–5, their commitment was £400,000 a season and, by then, in addition to the Regal Trophy, the Stones Bitter Championship and Premiership, and John Smith's support of Great Britain's Test series, a total of £1,625,000 was raised by the major sponsorship deals. According to Rodney Walker, chairman of the Rugby League, the higher national profile that he feels will come from the Super League should enable the game to attract money from major companies outside the traditional areas of drink and tobacco. 'Even if our government doesn't ban cigarette sponsorship, Brussels will, and we need to be prepared for that,' he said. 'Super League, and the improved image of the game, gives us the chance to widen the net and go after big national companies.' The first fruits of this policy came with the sponsorship of the 1995 World Cup by the Halifax Building Society. Whether the Halifax felt they had got value for their money, given the BBC's scant coverage of the tournament, is another matter. None the less, rugby league's visibility as a TV sport, added to the clearly defined social and regional profile of its followers, has made it an attractive proposition for sponsors. And in the same way that the sport's recent history has been punctuated by a series of brave enterprises that have gone awry, so there is a catalogue of knock-out tournaments that are no longer extant – the Captain Morgan Trophy, the Floodlit Trophy, the county cups which pre-date the formation of the league, the top-16 play-off (although the Premiership is its close relation), and various made-for-TV events, going back to ITA's floodlit competition in the Fifties.

The arrival of significant contributions from sponsorship in the early Seventies coincided with a change of personality and direction at the game's headquarters that was to have a far-reaching and long-lasting effect. Bill Fallowfield OBE had been secretary of the Rugby League for almost thirty years when he retired in 1974. While he presided over a period when the sport seemed to be in terminal decline and, in his latter years, drew much criticism for his apparent inability to recognize the seriousness of falling standards on and off the field, Fallowfield had been in his early career a pioneer who often led his colleagues kicking and screaming into a new era. This was particularly true with respect to the embracing of television, which many saw as simply having an adverse effect on attendances. In 1962, he wrote: 'Even those who most bitterly oppose the League's policy of televising games must learn to appreciate that, whether we like it or not, television is here to stay. It is up to us to make the best of it. During a period when the public absents itself from the terraces, surely it is a good policy to keep the game fresh in their minds. In this way they remember how it is played and they get acquainted with the stars of the game, so that they feel quite at home when once again they attend in person.' While there is something of a charming naivety in this view, there is little doubt that rugby league needed television just as much as television needed it.

The very fact that it was seen as a national TV sport was an important development, even though the BBC's attitude to the game was often a hindrance to progress. The commentary style of the late Eddie Waring, with his bizarrely nasal Ee-Bah-Gum, Up-'n'-Under and They-all-go-in-one-big-bath-here-at-Wigan declarations, was seen by some to give rugby league a profile somewhere in between clog dancing and *It's a Knock-out*. The presentation itself was invariably of dubious quality, poor direction and decidedly amateur camerawork (although, admittedly, conditions at the grounds were often primitive) heightening the sense that the BBC did not take the game seriously. The tone of the coverage had only one minor benefit. An Eddie Waring impersonation was part of the staple diet of impressionists from Mike Yarwood downwards in the early Seventies and although on one level this held the man and his sport up to ridicule, at least it did, in modern marketing-speak, raise awareness.

Waring became a joke and, in the eyes of devotees, a pretty bad one. By the time he belatedly retired in 1981, he was a deep embarrassment, a sadly out-of-date music-hall turn. It was a shame that Waring had been allowed to descend into self-parody, as he was capable of inspired moments. When Wakefield's Don Fox – having missed his last-second kick in front of the posts that would have won the 1968 Cup Final – sank traumatically to the Wembley turf, Waring's heartfelt 'Poor, poor, lad' was simple perfection. It deserves to be rated alongside Kenneth Wolstenholme's 'They think it's all over . . .' from the 1966 World Cup Final. In his final years, Waring failed, often literally, to keep up with the game, and his inability to refer to the Widnes hooker Keith Elwell without pre-fixing his name with the adjective 'ubiquitous' was only the most tolerable of his many idiosyncrasies.

The fact that the BBC would never have presented any other major sport – and certainly not rugby union – in such a patronizing and haphazard manner only served to fuel the feeling that there was an anti-northern bias in establishment circles, a view that has had currency ever since 1895. Nevertheless, television gave a northern game national exposure, was crucial in attracting sponsors and, until Rupert Murdoch and Sky came along, had only a limited influence on changing its structure.

Fallowfield had other sound views. He also wrote in 1962: 'Many people feel that the play-the-ball law needs urgent attention. Others see a good game of rugby league football and then state emphatically "there is nothing wrong with the laws if they are applied properly". What they will not appreciate is that the law can still be applied "properly" . . . but a team can still "stick the ball up its jersey" if it is so inclined. Personally, I think it is easy enough to think of solutions to this particular difficulty. The major obstacle is to obtain a two-thirds majority in favour of any one solution.' Given that the limited-tackle rule, a landmark change for the game, was not introduced until four years later, Fallowfield could be viewed as something of a visionary. As can be deduced from his closing statement, he was also in favour of modernizing the decision-making process. At that time, all major decisions were made by the thirty clubs, with a labyrinthine network of committees and sub-committees. 'From its inception, the League has been governed by the major clubs,' he wrote, 'and this is hardly conducive to producing a streamlined organization capable of accepting every opportunity for expansion and creating opportunity where none would otherwise exist.' It was a decade after Fallowfield wrote these words that a ten-man executive committee, headed by Ronnie Simpson, the league's chairman, was given responsibility for governing the sport, even though the big decisions had to be referred to the full council of clubs. Today, it is a six-man board of directors which wields the power.

Fallowfield, like Waring, had been allowed to go on too long. By 1974 he was an old man, exhausted by the unequal struggle and, unsurprisingly, bereft of fresh ideas. An abrasive character who had no gift for public relations, he was seen as remote and authoritarian by rugby league followers, and increasingly became the focus of their dissatisfaction with the lack of direction of the game. Within headquarters, his single-minded determination to prosecute his own beliefs was interpreted as arrogance and intransigence. On his retirement after twenty-eight years in the job, Bill Fallowfield would not have topped a popularity poll. The search for his successor was undertaken by the executive committee and when the short list was drawn up, the man at the head of the betting list was the former Leeds player Bev Risman, a college lecturer, one of a rugby league dynasty and a respected figure among players, administrators and supporters.

The final interviews were conducted in April 1974 by a cabal of nine former chairmen of the league. The last man to meet the panel late in the day was the most unlikely candidate; David Oxley, a deputy headmaster from the Duke of York's Military School in Dover. Oxley, although he had been born in Hull and had a solid rugby league background, was an Oxford graduate and had played union. In many ways, he was the polar opposite to Fallowfield. An erudite, well-spoken thirty-six-year-old, he brought with him a batch of fresh ideas and his application for the job – a two-page letter in which, under ten headings, he suggested ways for the game to move forward – excited the interest of two of the prime movers on the panel, Brian Snape (chairman of Salford) and Tom Mitchell (his counterpart at Workington). After an animated forty-minute interview, Oxley left a positive impression and, although he was told later that the chairmen had made their decision on the spot, it was three weeks before he was formally appointed to the job at a starting annual salary of £4,500.

There was no handover period – 'I had been a schoolteacher on the Friday and secretary of the Rugby League on Monday,' recalled Oxley – and his arrival at headquarters in Chapeltown Road, a run-down building in a run-down area of Leeds, left him in little doubt about the amateurish organization of the sport, or of the size of the task ahead. 'What immediately struck me,' Oxley explained, 'was the poor morale of those around me. The first thing one of my assistants said to me was: "I don't know why you've taken the job. We won't be around in a few years' time." I felt that the immediate priority was to restore confidence in the game.' His second cause for concern was his immediate environment. 'The Chapeltown Road offices contributed to the general air of depression. We desperately needed to smarten them up. The council chamber was nothing more than an office, and when meetings took place, tatty card tables and rickety chairs were brought in. A table with sandwiches was laid out in the corridor. It was a pretty seedy place at that time.' Oxley said that when league officials met prospective sponsors, they were taken to a hotel in Leeds. 'We couldn't let them anywhere near Chapeltown Road,' Oxley said. His initial appointment was that of the game's first public relations officer, a twenty-two-year-old *Hull Daily Mail* news journalist, David Howes, who was also shocked by the seriousness of the situation. 'At that time,' he said, 'the game was as close as it could be to going under. All the hatches were battened down, and there was the smell of death all around.'

Together, they undertook an exhaustive tour of rugby league towns, accepting any invitation that came their way, soliciting others, addressing supporters' meetings, and talking to anyone who would listen. It was the first stage in what Oxley called 'humanizing the game'. 'Our immediate impression was one of deep gloom. Everyone seemed to think the game was dying. But their feelings to us were not hostile. In fact, they appeared to be sympathetic to these two idiots, sitting there taking all the flak. We had to remind them that this was their game, and they had a big stake in it. It was very instructive, and good fun. I remember one night at Barrow when the split with Barla [the British Amateur Rugby League Association] was the subject of a long and heated debate. At the end, one chap stood up and asked: "Who is this bloke Barlow who's creating all the trouble?" Attendances at most of the meetings exceeded our expectations and it was a big step in the right direction.' Howes said: 'We didn't have a formulated plan. We set out in a spirit of blind optimism, and were basically just going around banging the drum. But it was like blowing up a tyre; everywhere we went, we pumped a bit more air into the game.' It was a wearying process, particularly for Howes, as Oxley couldn't drive. 'We covered thousands and thousands of miles,' said Howes. 'Once, on our way from Leeds to a meeting at Keighley, we stopped for a rest at a pub in Bingley. Five minutes later, we were both fast asleep in our chairs and the landlord had to wake us up. But we had to open up the game, and the effort was well worth it.' The only casualty was Howes's new Triumph 1500, whose engine was not as robust as its owner's.

With Oxley as a highly effective front man, and Howes, in his amiable bluff manner, cultivating branches of the media (on a national, as well as regional, basis), the game at last had a plausible public relations operation. They were supported in their initiatives by one of the game's rare forward-thinkers who, in 1974, became the league chairman. Brian Snape, a hotel, restaurant and bingo hall owner, had become the buccaneering chairman of Salford in 1965, taking over from his father, who had held the post for thirty years. Snape was the original entrepreneur of the modern era; he thought big and bought big. At one end of Salford's compact ground, the Willows, he built a low-level social club which not only made a huge financial contribution but helped create a more glamorous image for what had been until that time a truly unglamorous club. Snape's grand ideas were made flesh by a succession of major signings.

None of his purchases had as dramatic an effect as David Watkins, the Newport and Wales rugby union stand-off who turned professional in October 1967 for a signing-on fee of

£10,000, plus £1,000 at the start of the succeeding five seasons. His first appearance for Salford was in a home match against Oldham on a Friday night. (Snape's decision to move Salford's fixtures to Friday night had been successful; the floodlit games had an element of theatre that attracted many of the floating voters among the Manchester sporting public.) In his autobiography written in 1980, Watkins tells of his immediate impression on arriving in the city of Salford: 'Demolition and slum clearances have changed the face of this part of the world in the past decade. But in 1967, all you could see from the road were row upon row of tiny, terraced houses garlanded by lines of washing, hanging not in the gardens, for there were none, but across what appeared to be main streets. "This is hell," I was saying frankly to myself. "It makes the South Wales valleys seem like Utopia".'

A capacity crowd of almost 15,000, swelled by coachloads from Wales, was present to see Watkins make his debut. It was a night alive with expectation, the first of many such occasions at the Willows. Watkins scored two drop-goals and a try, breaking clear in his own 25 and scampering all the way to the line, in an 11–6 victory. It was an ominously impressive first appearance. Watkins switched to play in the centre and then at full-back and, after sixteen years in the game, he could lay serious claim to being the most successful convert ever from union; he holds five club scoring records, was the league's leading points scorer three seasons in succession, is the only player ever to have played and scored in every game for two whole seasons, and his 221 goals in the 1972–3 campaign remains the highest total in a season. In addition to Watkins, Salford captured several other leading union internationals – Keith Fielding and Mike Coulman from England and the Welshman Maurice Richards. With these were blended a number of established league players as, four times between 1968 and 1975, Salford broke the record transfer fee. The rewards were tangible; crowds regularly topped five figures, the First Division Championship was won twice, and in addition to claiming the Lancashire Cup and the Floodlit Trophy, Salford reached Wembley in 1969 for the first time, but were beaten by Castleford. Salford's floodlit experience pointed the way forward. 'In many aspects,' said David Oxley, 'what Salford did in the late Sixties and early Seventies was a prototype for Wigan in the Eighties and Nineties.'

Snape had shown, with a mixture of vision, drive, ambition and a pile of cash, what was possible. It was the end of the Seventies before this example was followed, when the game took off as never before in the city of Hull. Even before that remarkable explosion, there were signs that, under Oxley's modern style of leadership, the slump in fortunes were beginning to be reversed. The 1977–8 season ended with attendances at last showing an increase and, significantly, the column inches in national newspapers that Howes totted up on a daily basis had risen considerably. Feedback was positive. The season ended with an exciting Cup Final in which Leeds beat St Helens and, after the match, Oxley met Bob Weighill, his counterpart at Twickenham. 'Bob came up to me and said that it was a superb game and that I must be very pleased with the way things are going. It was the first time I stood back and reflected that maybe we were on the right track.'

Oxley continued to press forward with a quiet revolution of the game's structure, and many of the important decisions regarding forward planning, commercial management and ground development devolved away from the full council of clubs to the executive committee. Some of the marketing initiatives betrayed a certain unworldliness; 'A man's game for all the family' was a slogan invented to promote the game's earthy but wholesome virtues. Yet Howes's more direct methods of courting the press – through chipping away at the perceived prejudices of sports editors – and the public – with an entertaining and provocative roadshow – were highly effective.

It was the phenomenon on Humberside, however, that helped give rugby league the national exposure it craved. Interest in rugby league in the city had been dormant in the Seventies, but competition between the two clubs divided by the River Humber – to the west, the black-and-white favours of Hull FC, and to the east, the red-and-white of Hull Kingston Rovers – had always been intense, a small-scale version of the rivalries of soccer such as Manchester United and City, Liverpool and Everton or Sheffield Wednesday and United. In the Fifties and early Sixties, Hull FC, had enjoyed the ascendancy, but by the Seventies positions were reversed and there was a pall of depression hanging over Hull's ground, The Boulevard. (The name may suggest an exotic location. It was anything but, and the title of its famous enclosure – a wooden structure called 'The Threepenny Stand' – gives a more accurate flavour of the venue's humble charms.) David Oxley recalled that, on the night after he had his interview in 1974, he went to watch a match at the Boulevard. 'There were 1100 people there, and the atmosphere was deadly. It was a salutary experience, and I knew then the fearful extent of the game's problems.' Four years later, an astounding transformation had been wrought that revived Hull FC, had a knock-on effect on Rovers, put the city on the sporting map, and played a large role in the regeneration of rugby league.

In 1978, a boardroom coup at Hull led to the appointment of a millionaire enthusiast, Roy Waudby, as chairman. Waudby had made his fortune from a shopping credit card and his watchwords – in rugby league, at least – were spend, spend and spend. The club had just been relegated to the Second Division, but a series of expensive, yet extremely astute signings, helped create a team that cut a record-breaking swathe through the division. Hull won the Second Division championship without losing one of their twenty-six games, scoring 702 points, attracting an average home crowd of almost 7,000 while their massive travelling support gave every club they visited their highest attendance of the season. With both Hull clubs now in the First Division, and Rovers responding to their rivals' initiative with big signings of their own, the 1979–80 season saw a further explosion of interest. Hull finished in third position in the First Division, Rovers a few places below, but it was the crowd figures that provided the most impressive statistics; Hull finished the season with an average of a little more than 10,000, while Rovers' was almost 7,000, some 1,000 up on the previous year. They were easily the two best-supported teams in the league. It was a phenomenon that did not go unnoticed beyond the Humber. In March 1980, Phil Shaw wrote in the *Observer*: 'The city of Hull is unique. Apart from its white telephone boxes, it is the only place in the country where rugby league is beating soccer hands down in the battle for the hearts and wallets of the paying public . . . With three home games left, Hull have established a First Division aggregate attendance record – 119,856 have passed through their turnstiles, including 20,000 for the Humberside Derby.'

The season built to a suitable climax, when the teams met at Wembley for the first ever all-Humberside Cup Final. Not surprisingly, it attracted a capacity crowd of 95,000, and when the vast armies of supporters left the city on the journey to London, they were greeted by a sign that read: 'Will the last one to leave please turn off the lights'. Hull KR won a tense match 10–5 to claim the trophy for the first time in their history. In five of the next six seasons, one of the two Hull clubs contested the Wembley final, although the only success fell to Hull, who beat Widnes after a replay in 1982. The 1982 *Rugby League Yearbook* said that 'Hull confirmed their status as the best supported club in the world,' and new attendance records continued to be set, including one that still stands: the 25,165 for a John Player Trophy Final between the two clubs.

The renaissance on Humberside was almost entirely

responsible for the healthier appearance of crowd figures for the game as a whole. From the 1977–8 season, when the aggregate league attendance rose for the first time in the decade, until 1982–3, there was steady progress each year. There was another dip until 1985–6, by which time the boom at Hull had begun to fizzle out, and Wigan, whose average crowds had risen from 7,429 to 12,515 in just two seasons, assumed the position of dominance that remains unchallenged. Wembley in 1985 represented the changing of the guard. In possibly the greatest Cup Final ever, Wigan defeated Hull 28–24, the match a showcase for the sublime talents of some of the world's best rugby players. Derek Wyatt, a former England rugby union international wrote later: 'I have only seen a handful of rugby league games, one of which was the 1985 Challenge Cup Final between Wigan and Hull. A contest that was so enthralling, so exciting, so full of skill and imagination that I was moved to write that it was better than the Barbarians versus the All Blacks classic at the Arms Park in those heady days of 1973 when British rugby union, for once, stood supreme.' Frank Keating, in the *Guardian*, was equally effusive, describing it as 'the most voluptuous exhibition of rugby it has ever been my privilege to witness'. David Howes felt that the match was 'a landmark. It was the one game that captured people's imagination at a national level.'

The combined effects of the economic recession and ground safety regulations instituted after the Bradford City fire of 1985 and the Hillsborough disaster four years later had a profound effect throughout rugby league, but dealt an especially grave blow to the Hull clubs. Available resources had to be spent on patching up their ageing grounds – Hull were forced to shut down their 'Threepenny Stand' – and there was no money to be spent on team-building to meet the challenge of Wigan. Hull had to sell their chief assets – internationals such as Garry Schofield and Lee Crooks, who both joined Leeds – while Hull KR were eventually forced to leave their Craven Park ground. Doubling up as a greyhound stadium, it was one of the league's less attractive venues, but the new Craven Park is an even more cheerless place, a featureless modern ground close to the docks and prey to the wind whipping in off the North Sea. The halcyon days of the early Eighties now seem like a distant illusion on Humberside, and when the Super League came along, Hull were in the First Division while Rovers were in the Second and, in 1994–5, the combined average crowd of the two was barely more than 6,000. The cyclical nature of sporting success, plus the vibrant state of the amateur game in the city, dictates that one or both of the Hull clubs are bound to strike out again for the summit.

If events in Hull in the early Eighties helped put rugby league on the national sporting agenda, the arrival in 1982 of the finest touring party from either code to hit these shores since the original All Blacks of 1905 washed away the last residues of prejudice about the quality of the game at its highest level. The record of the fifteenth Australian tourists tells its own story; played 15, won 15, points for 423, points against 80, scoring 97 tries and conceding a mere seven. In 10 of their 15 matches, they scored 27 points or more. But it was the quality of their play, their speed and fitness levels, their imaginative attacking and indomitable defence, the all-round skills of players in every position, that attracted attention from both sides of the rugby divide. The late Carwyn James, former coach of Wales and the British Lions rugby union sides, wrote in the *Guardian* that the Kangaroos had 'restored the art of collision rugby allied to support play which leads to sustained, thrilling movements'. League men were no less impressed. Alex Murphy declared that they 'were from another planet', while Phil Larder, then the newly appointed national director of coaching and later to become coach of Great Britain for the 1995 World Cup campaign, said, 'The tourists were far in advance of the British in every aspect of the game, and the more their performances are studied, the greater the difference is seen to be.'

It was a traumatic few months for the British game, whose poverty of ideas and staleness of approach had been exposed in terrible fashion. For some, it came as no surprise. 'The warning signs had been clear to see,' said David Oxley. 'On the 1978 tour, the final Test at Headingley [Australia's youthful side won more convincingly than the 23–6 margin of victory suggested] provided a clear indication that our standards were lagging some way behind theirs. But at that time, the international game was not taken as seriously as it should have been, and it was difficult to get people to accept that the problem should be addressed.' In the succeeding four years, Britain stood still while Australia moved further forward. Even then, many in the British game often expressed the simplistic and outdated belief that while Australian players had superior physique, our players had the edge in skill and finesse. The first Test of the 1982 series shattered this illusion for ever. In beating Britain 40–4 in front of a near capacity crowd at Hull City's football ground and millions watching live TV coverage, Australia laid out their manifesto for rugby of the future. The second half, which saw the Australians score thirty points without reply, was a flawless exhibition of the running game, the basic skills of handling, passing and support play elevated to something near an art form. As the procession over the British line developed, the crowd watched at first in awed silence but, by the end, were generous in their appreciation. They gave the tourists a standing ovation as they left the field.

For those present, it was a revelation. As Paul Fitzpatrick wrote in the *Rugby League Review*: 'Practically every move threatened a try; their finishing was ruthless and every move, every try was a demonstration of their superiority over the British. The true width of the divide between the countries was beginning at last to be appreciated.' Britain's response was to make ten changes for the second Test, while the coach Maurice Bamford, in the misguided belief that a surge of nationalism might make up for technical shortcomings, made some of his players carry a Union Jack flag to each of the four corners of the Central Park pitch before the game. It was the desperate act of desperate men. Despite the sending-off in the first half of Les Boyd, a prop whose indiscipline was in sharp contrast to his team-mates, the Australians won 27–6. They may have been twelve men against thirteen, but the imbalance in quality between the sides more than made up for their numerical disadvantage and, again, Britain failed to score a try. Once more, the spectators were lost in wonder for the tourists. 'Rarely in sport can a team have won such ungrudging admiration from their opponents' supporters,' wrote Fitzpatrick.

The final Test at Headingley provided Britain with their first reason for optimism. The Kangaroos won 32–8, but eighteen of their points came in the final ten minutes and at last their line was breached, Hull's centre Steve Evans joining an exclusive club of only seven players who scored a try against the Australians during the entire tour. 'It was a true Test,' said the tourists' normally taciturn coach, Frank Stanton. Some of those who caused such damage returned to play for British clubs – Brett Kenny, who went on to win the Lance Todd trophy at Wembley with Wigan; Peter Sterling, the dynamic blond scrum-half who joined Hull; Wally Lewis, the masterly stand-off who led the scarcely less impressive 1986 tourists, had a brief spell with Wakefield Trinity; and Mal Meninga, the unstoppable centre with hands like shovels, had an unforgettable season at St Helens. But their most significant legacy was to force the British game into re-evaluation. 'Even the blindest of the blind had to admit it,' said David Oxley. 'We were miles behind. And we were forced to do a lot of soul-searching. In many ways, that tour was a turning point.' More resources were poured into the national coaching scheme, club coaches began to use the modern training methods pioneered by the Australians, efforts were directed into raising the level of refereeing, and greater attention was paid to the youth game.

The modern history of both codes of rugby have, in part, been shaped by the 1982 Kangaroos. Not only did they point the direction forward for British rugby league but, in attracting such attention, they provided a lead for international rugby union, a game which, in the northern hemisphere at least, had become bereft of ideas and stultifyingly inhibited. The first to absorb the lessons were, not surprisingly, the Australian rugby union team, at that time under the forward-looking direction of the coach Alan Jones. When the Wallabies arrived in Britain in 1984, their expansive style, with the accent on slick handling and tireless support play, was reminiscent of their professional compatriots of two years previously. So was their record; an historic grand slam of victories against the four home nations, scoring a hundred points in the process and conceding only thirty-three. They also inspired an outbreak of self-analysis in our domestic game, but even as rugby union entered the professional era in 1995, the approach in British rugby union still tends towards the conservative. When England were comprehensively dismantled by New Zealand in the 1995 World Cup, Jack Rowell, the shell-shocked England manager, said afterwards of the All Blacks: 'They play like a rugby league side.' It was a remarkable, some may say treacherous, statement, but was none the less true. And the rugby league side they played like, Rowell might have added, were the '82 Kangaroos.

When the 1986 Kangaroos arrived in Britain, they encountered a more vibrant challenge. Even though they were again undefeated on the short thirteen-match tour, achieving another clean sweep in the Test series, there were signs that the self-examination which followed the 1982 experience had been translated into a raising of standards. Wigan, who by now dominated the domestic game, were only beaten by eight points, Oldham got even closer, losing 22–16, and in the final Test at Wigan, Great Britain went the distance before a late Australian try gave them a 24–15 victory. Of equal importance were the crowds drawn by the Kangaroos; 30,622 for the visit to Wigan, a record for a club game on tour, and 50,383 to Old Trafford for the First Test, the highest attendance for an international in this country. The average crowd of 16,313 was second only to the 1948 tour.

Australian examples were followed by Wigan, under the enlightened chairmanship of Maurice Lindsay and the direction of coach Graham Lowe, a New Zealander. They set the standards in every aspect of the game; professionalism on and off the field (they were the first club to have full-time pros and their wage bill is comparable to some Premiership football clubs), crowds (they have not had an season's average of lower than 10,000 for more than a decade), marketing and merchandising, and, tying up cause and effect, their playing record (by the end of the 1994–5 season, they had finished top of the First Division seven seasons in succession and had extended their domination of the Challenge Cup to eight years). They also gave the first real indication that the gap between Britain and Australia was narrowing when, in 1987 before 36,895 at Central Park, they defeated Manly, the Australian Grand Final champions, 8–2 in a World Club Challenge match.

A year later, Great Britain completed the leap when, on an unforgettable day at the Sydney Cricket Ground, they beat Australia 26–12 in the Third Test to bring to an end a sequence of fifteen consecutive defeats. Succeeding series have followed a similar trend, with Britain winning one battle but losing the war. In 1990, the Australians were beaten at Wembley; at Melbourne in 1992, Britain claimed a remarkable 33–10 victory; in 1994, a try by Jonathan Davies gave Britain an 8–4 triumph, again at Wembley. And in the 1995 World Cup, it was one victory apiece, Britain winning the opening game of the tournament but Australia, drastically weakened by their refusal to select players who had signed up for the Super League, triumphed in the one that mattered, the Final. By taking the trophy with what was effectively their reserve team, Australia demonstrated the strength of their domestic league; by showing, over this competition and the previous three series, that they could now compete on roughly equal terms, Britain had proved just how far our game has travelled since the humiliation of 1982.

In 1992, David Oxley retired, as he said he would, at the age of fifty-five. He was replaced, the post now that of chief executive, by Maurice Lindsay, the guiding hand behind Wigan. Simply judged, Oxley's period in charge had been a successful one; the game was in a healthier state when he departed than when he joined. There had been positive gains: the dismantling of an unwieldy decision-making process; the largely successful public relations offensive; a more outward-looking, open style of government; a more enlightened policy towards the recruitment and training of referees; and the establishment of a national coaching structure (albeit more than a decade after the Australians). But while there was no longer dry rot at Chapeltown Road, neither was there cause for self-congratulation. The missionary zeal of the Eighties – which saw success in Sheffield, survival against the odds in London and Carlisle, but abject failure in Cardiff, Maidstone, Scarborough, Nottingham, Runcorn and Trafford – was replaced with worries much closer to home. The implementation of the directives of the Taylor Report into the Hillsborough disaster, spiralling wage bills and the deepening recession left even those clubs established in the First Division in a state of penury. Overall playing standards had never been higher, money from sponsorship and television deals was rolling in at a record rate, but a majority of clubs relied on hand-outs from the league and bank loans to stay alive. And a visit to all but a handful of venues was not a cheering experience. Facilities for spectators were, at best, basic, and the parlous condition of many grounds was hindering the game's attempts to present a bright, modern image to the world.

Lindsay took over a sport that had made substantial advances in the Eighties, but was nevertheless in a financial mire. One of his first moves was to engage a sports consultancy company to investigate the nature and depth of the problems. They presented their grim findings in the autumn of 1994. The clubs were told that, if the game was to survive, many difficult issues had to be confronted. Six months later, Rupert Murdoch was on the telephone.

FIVE

FAST REALITY

The birth of the Super League

When rugby league and Rupert Murdoch walked off arm in arm in the spring of 1995, it was neither simplistic nor convenient to believe that they had both reached the same crossroads at the same time, but by altogether different routes.

Rugby league, a game born through the financial needs of its players almost exactly a hundred years earlier, found itself in difficult times. Most of its thirty-two professional clubs (all but one of which were based in the economically depressed north of England) were living on or below the breadline; a succession of initiatives designed to broaden the game's base by establishing clubs in uncharted territory had met with limited success; the introduction of players' contracts in 1989 had massively increased wage bills and was threatening to drive some clubs out of business; most grounds were in a state of serious disrepair while some belonged in another age. In addition, the league was being dominated by one club, Wigan, who, by the end of the 1995 season, had won the Challenge Cup eight years in succession, as well as monopolizing almost every other trophy.

Maurice Lindsay, the former chairman of Wigan, found himself having to find solutions to these problems when he took over as the league's chief executive in 1992. In 1993, with the financial help of the sport's main sponsor, Bass Brewers, he commissioned a Leeds-based marketing company, GSM, to undertake a major examination of the game and to present recommendations for its survival and development. The research took almost a year, and in the autumn of 1994, a document entitled 'Framing the Future' was laid before the clubs. It presented a bleak picture. Too many clubs were fighting for too few spectators in too small a catchment area – 60 per cent of all those who attended professional games came from just four postal districts in the M62 corridor; facilities at grounds were woefully inadequate; many clubs were said to be living in a financial 'fool's paradise', spending more than they could afford in pursuit of success and running up huge debts in the process; and insufficient regard was given to marketing the game. While much of the evidence hardly came as a shock to the gathering, the obvious conclusions were less easily digested, particularly the suggestion that there should be a Premier League with fewer clubs, and that mergers could make better use of the limited resources available. It was the first time that those involved in running rugby league had been forced to address such fundamental questions, and the debate was now in the public arena.

At the meeting of the rugby league council (at which each professional club has a representative) that followed the presentation, Lindsay converted some of the general points in the report into financial specifics: of the thirty-two clubs, seventeen were technically insolvent, and while there had been a 3 per cent growth in gross income over the previous three years, players' wages had increased by 10 per cent. He added that clubs were selling their grounds at 'an alarming rate', and this was an option that could be exercised only once. The grim warnings were absorbed. Gary Hetherington, the chairman of Sheffield Eagles said that 'history will not solve the problems of the future', and Denis Greenwood, his counterpart at Leeds, added that there was 'too much sentiment and tradition in rugby league. A more commercial view was needed.' There was even discussion about whether a breakaway league may be the result of the game at large failing to grasp its problems, while, on the subject of summer rugby, Lindsay said that it could not be implemented for at least two years because of television and sponsorship contracts.

The arrival of Rupert Murdoch on to the scene six months later was to render this dialogue irrelevant. A global magnate with newspaper and television interests in the two major centres of rugby league, Great Britain and Australia, Murdoch had seen the commercial benefit to his subscription TV channels of securing the rights to major sporting events. (His ground-breaking contract to secure live coverage to the First Division of the English Football League, which resulted in the founding of the FA Premiership in 1988, transformed the fortunes of his Sky satellite channel in the UK.) Sky already owned the rights to the rugby league championship, broadcasting live matches on Friday nights and highlights on Sundays, but, if he could seize control of the sport, Murdoch sensed an opportunity to dominate the market closest to his heart – Australia.

Rugby league is the only game that matters in Australia, or at least in the major population centres in New South Wales and Queensland. The generally held view that a market the size of Australia would support only one subscription TV channel meant that the purchase of the rights to a substantial sporting property would not only provide a significant boost for his own Channel 9 but would deal a grievous blow to his major rival Kerry Packer, who at the time owned the rights to the domestic Australian game.

Murdoch decided to go for global hegemony, offering the game in Britain and Australia wealth beyond imagination and the chance to realize a long-held ambition to turn rugby league into a major player on the world sporting stage. The plan, at its most basic, was to have a Super League structure in both countries. As it developed, the seasons would run concurrently (meaning that the British game would move to the summer) and the climax of the campaign would be a knock-out tournament involving the top teams from each league. Naturally, the television rights would be held exclusively by the respective Murdoch channels. Early in 1995, an approach was made to the Australian Rugby League, whose officials remained faithful to their contract with Packer and rebuffed Murdoch. He then opted for a more direct approach to the clubs themselves and to individual players, and was successful in signing up much of the talent in the world's strongest league. As well as securing the services of individual players, he bought up entire teams. The Packer-backed ARL launched a counter-offensive, competing by offering equally huge contracts for home-based players and looking towards the stars in the British game. Hostilities had been opened, and the battle ended up in court.

Maurice Lindsay was in Sydney for the World Sevens tournament on the weekend of 4 February and kept a close watching brief on the machinations that were to leave the Australian game riven by discord. At the March meeting of the Rugby League Council, he warned British clubs that what was happening down under was bound to have an effect on the domestic game. It was a month later that the first contact with the Murdoch organization was established. When it came, it was a deal that made sense for many of the men who held the power in the British game. The Murdoch money over five years would be a financial lifebelt for many clubs, and could be used to upgrade stadiums and improve facilities. Furthermore, here was a chance, after many years of trying, for the game to break free from its northern redoubt and achieve the wider recognition that its proponents felt it clearly deserved. But to many others, particularly among the game's long-suffering supporters, it was a contract of Faustian infelicity. Murdoch did not seek to purchase television rights; he wanted to buy the game itself.

The move to playing in the summer was one of the less contentious proposals, although it meant farewell to peering through the mist, to grounds ankle-deep in mud, to steam rising from scrums like geysers, to hot pies on freezing afternoons and to the traditional Boxing Day Derby matches. All these aspects may have added to the game's atmospheric attraction but, in age when competition for the public's 'leisure-spend' is intense, there is no room for sentimentality and the game cannot be frozen in a grainy black-and-white image for ever. Its appeal to spectators can only increase if the danger of frost-bite is eliminated and the decision to move to a more clement season might have been taken by the clubs themselves even if Murdoch had not shown up.

Jim Quinn, chairman of Oldham: 'I had been campaigning for a switch to summer for three years. At first, I met a lot of resistance. In 1994, we played Wigan at Watersheddings [Oldham's hilltop ground is possibly the most exposed in the entire league] and the conditions were absolutely atrocious. It was doing the lot, snowing, blowing a gale, and some of the players had to be treated for hypothermia. As he came off the pitch, the Wigan player Joe Lydon said to me: "Whatever you do, Jim, keep bloody fighting for summer rugby." But in the boardroom afterwards, the Wigan chairman Jack Robinson stood up and said: "This is real rugby league, it's a proper game. It's a winter sport, and should stay so." Twelve months later, he had changed his mind. I thought then that someone had been talking to him, that something was afoot.'

Quinn had presented a report to rugby league officials on the case for summer rugby back in late 1992, but had been frustrated by the apparent lack of action on the matter. His most vociferous supporters were the chairmen of Bradford Northern and Sheffield Eagles.

Quinn: 'I saw Maurice Lindsay after we had been beaten by Wigan in the Challenge Cup semi-final in March 1995. We talked about summer rugby. I said that unless someone comes in and bangs the table with a lump of money, it'll never happen. His reply was: "We're down the road ahead of you. Wait and see." I was then asked to present my proposals for a switch to summer at the quarterly council meeting at Headingley on Wednesday 5 April.'

Unbeknown to his colleagues, Lindsay came to the meeting armed with a more serious proposal. The previous day, at 11.10 a.m., he had taken a telephone call from Sam Chisholm, the chief executive of the BSkyB satellite channel, in his office in Leeds. Chisholm invited Lindsay to talks in London that day to discuss the possibility of a Super League deal. Lindsay left rugby league headquarters in the afternoon and arrived at Chisholm's west London apartment at eight in the evening. As he entered the apartment block, he saw the boxing promoter Frank Warren leaving. A deal had just been done with Warren; time to move on to another one. Lindsay was met by Chisholm, Vic Wakeling, the head of sport on BSkyB, and Tony Ball, then the business manager of Sky Sports. Lindsay recalled: 'Chisholm said, quite directly: "You know we have done a Super League deal with Australia. Are you in?" I told him it was not quite as easy as that, and asked him what he meant. We talked for about two hours on the ramifications. No money was mentioned, but I told him that we were to have a Council meeting the next day and that summer rugby was on the agenda.'

'It was a general discussion,' said Vic Wakeling, 'about the complexities of moving to a summer season. It moved on to a business level. At that time, there was a chance that one or both of the rival organizations in Australia could come over here and sign up our best players. A sport that was already in trouble was in danger of going to the wall. If the top names had gone to Australia, what would be left here? Broad agreement was reached at that meeting to make the Super League work. We didn't really discuss mergers, although I suggested that I thought it was madness that there were two clubs in a big city like Hull and neither of them was in the top division.'

The common perception was that the impetus for switching to the summer came from Murdoch's organization; Lindsay claims this not to be the case. 'They actually wanted us to stay in the winter, but I told him that if we moved to the summer, it would dovetail nicely with the Australian season. I still wasn't sure that summer rugby would be supported. I knew there would be resistance from the traditionalists, and I wasn't sure in my own mind either. But slowly I began to be convinced by the argument. The one thing that persuaded me was a letter in one of the specialist magazines from an amateur coach. He said that those people who say that ours is a winter game have never stood out on a dark, freezing February night trying to coach twelve-year-old schoolboys whose sleeves are over their fingers, frozen to death, and you are trying to tell them how great the game is, and how to catch and pass the ball. That's it, I thought; it's not just the selfish ones who just want eighty minutes on a Sunday afternoon, it's everybody else. And that hit me like a thunderbolt. In my mind, I imagined Martin Offiah or Denis Betts in the middle of a field with loads of kids around them, the sun shining, everybody comfortable and happy, mothers on the touchline, and I began to think that this might work. I was sufficiently convinced to have voted for summer rugby at the Council meeting. But it certainly wasn't a requirement of News Corporation.' Nevertheless, Wakeling freely admits that, simply in terms of spreading Sky's major sports around the calendar, the move to summer was beneficial to his channel. After his meeting with Chisholm, Lindsay, his mind racing, stayed the night in a London hotel and took the first train back to Leeds to attend that morning's Council meeting. Over the telephone, he had already communicated the details of his discussions to Rodney

Walker, the chairman of the league. Before he arrived at Headingley, Lindsay took a call on his car phone from Ken Arthurson, chairman of the Australian Rugby League. Arthurson gave further details of the turmoil that Super League had caused down under and urged caution.

With these words fresh in his mind, Lindsay entered the meeting. Headingley, the famous back-to-back home of Leeds rugby league and Yorkshire cricket clubs, has seen its share of sporting history, but few who gathered in a banqueting suite overlooking the cricket pitch that afternoon were prepared for the drama that unfolded. Quinn opened his file of documents and was ready to launch his case which, from his own straw poll, looked certain to get the required two-thirds majority. With timing almost too perfect, Lindsay was summoned to answer a telephone call by one of the catering assistants and Jim Quinn held his fire. 'I went into the catering manager's office and on the phone was Sam Chisholm,' explained Lindsay. 'He said the boss wanted a word with me. I was slightly puzzled, but when he said that he was connecting me to Washington, I realized that, bloody hell, it must be Rupert Murdoch. Sam had obviously told him to give me a call to provide some reassurance. Murdoch said that he wanted us to know that they were very serious about this offer, and that the approach was a genuine one. He added that Chisholm has his personal backing and that I should communicate this to the clubs.'

Lindsay returned to the meeting room after fifteen minutes. 'Gentlemen,' he said, 'You are not going to believe this, but that was Rupert Murdoch.' He went on to outline, in broad terms, that News Corporation, the parent company of the Murdoch organization, had made a serious proposal to create a Super League and that, although no figures had been mentioned at this point, there would clearly be a substantial financial deal attached to it. He added that two of the interested parties – Barry Maranta of Brisbane Broncos, who had already thrown their lot in with the Super League, and David Smith, a News Corporation executive based in Australia – were at the Hilton Hotel in Leeds prepared to open talks. There was a move to have them address the meeting but it was eventually decided that Lindsay should be charged with finding out more details. 'What they really wanted to know was how much money was on the table,' Lindsay said. Rodney Walker said that the potential deal was 'a marvellous opportunity for the game as long as everyone remained united. The injection of capital would enable rugby league to be presented to the entire world as a professional sport for the first time.' The unity of the clubs was to be the first casualty as negotiations proceeded. But before the meeting was wrapped up, a vote was taken to gauge the support for summer rugby; only six out of thirty-three voted against.

That evening, Lindsay met Maranta and Smith and talked through the implications for the game on both continents. In the course of their discussion, Chisholm telephoned Lindsay and asked him to come to London by 8 a.m. the next day. Lindsay left Leeds on the 5 a.m. train, went straight to Chisholm's apartment and the two were taken by Chisholm's chauffeur to the BSkyB headquarters in Isleworth, west London. 'He asked about the previous day's Council meeting. I said that the mood had been positive but basically the clubs now wanted him to put some meat on the bone. What was the actual offer?' After some negotiation, Chisholm came up with £75 million. 'The magnitude of the offer was so mind-boggling', said Lindsay, 'that I was actually shaking a little bit. I knew how fragile the finances were in rugby league, and I believed this was a godsend for the game. Sam asked me how many teams would be in the league. I hesitantly suggested ten. That translated into £1.5 million a year for each.'

Lindsay shook hands with Chisholm and went straight to see Walker, who is also chairman of the Sports Council, at his office opposite Euston Station in London. 'We both sat there and shook our heads,' Lindsay said. 'We knew that as long as we didn't make a balls of it, we had a fantastic offer.' They considered the huge implications for the sport and discussed whether this might be a propitious time to bring about their desired objective of reducing the number of teams in the league. 'Sky wanted an elite competition,' explained Lindsay, 'but they didn't necessarily want excellence based on A joining with B. That was a matter for us, as was the matter of distributing the money. Rodney and I discussed how many teams were going to go into the pot. We knew we would have to offer a competition that was different from the existing sixteen-club championship.' Together, they worked out a plan that could be presented to the clubs. Lindsay then dictated a fax to his secretary in Leeds, asking all the major clubs to come to a meeting on Friday night, stressing the importance and the confidentiality of the business to be discussed. 'I did not think it was a divisive measure,' said Lindsay. 'These were the clubs who would be most affected by the deal.' He then dictated another fax to go to those not likely to be involved in the Super League to attend a meeting of all clubs at Wigan on Saturday morning. The fax stated, in bold type, that the representatives must be in a position to vote. 'This made it clear that they would be walking into a very serious meeting.' Almost exactly forty-eight hours from his first contact with Chisholm, Lindsay returned to Leeds unshakeably convinced that the deal he had negotiated would save rugby league.

On Friday morning, representatives of all First Division clubs received faxed notification of the meeting at the Hilton Hotel, Huddersfield to begin at 8 p.m. One Second Division club, Hull Kingston Rovers, were also invited. The meeting was opened by Walker (Lindsay arrived ten minutes late, having completed a television interview). For the first time, detailed plans were presented; by now, there was a written offer from News Corporation. The deal was worth £75 million over five years, and there was to be a summer Super League of fourteen clubs to include two from France (in Paris and Toulouse), one in London and one in Wales. The money on offer would commute to more than £1 million a season for five years for each of the Super League clubs. Excitement turned into high anxiety with the stunning proposal that not only was the league to be restructured – the move to summer having already been agreed with Chisholm – but the clubs themselves were, in modern industrial parlance, to be 'downsized'. More accurately, the Super League would include five new clubs to be created by the merging of fifteen existing ones.

It was decided that Castleford, Featherstone Rovers and Wakefield Trinity, three clubs from Yorkshire towns so close to each other that they could be covered by a 5p piece on an Ordnance Survey map and bitter adversaries on the rugby field, should combine to form a club by the name of Calder, after the river that runs through the West Yorkshire coalfield. Other plans included the fusing of the four clubs based in the north-west outpost – Barrow, Carlisle, Workington Town and Whitehaven – to create Cumbria; a Humberside team would be the result of a merger between Hull and Hull Kingston Rovers; Sheffield Eagles and Doncaster would melt into a South Yorkshire club and the coupling of Salford and Oldham would bring about a team called Manchester, a truly bizarre proposition given that neither club is based within the city's boundaries. The amalgamation of Warrington and Widnes, implacable rivals, to form a Cheshire club was discussed, but both stated their desire to stay independent, so Warrington were included and Widnes were named first reserve for a Super League place. Five other existing clubs – Wigan, St Helens, Halifax, Leeds and Bradford Northern – are to be given Super League places on their own. The representatives were told that a quick decision had to be made; the offer would be withdrawn if progress was not speedy.

Eddie Ashton, then the Castleford chairman: 'What gave

me a jolt was when Denis Greenwood, the Leeds chairman, said that, because of difficulties with the cricket at Headingley, there was no way that Leeds could contemplate summer rugby. He was told by Rodney Walker: "You're either in or you're out. And there's the door." It was as brutal as that. I thought that if they were prepared to treat a club as big as Leeds like that, we ought to give the idea of a merger consideration. But I never thought it was a possibility. Castleford and Featherstone people just don't mix.'

Geoff Fletcher, chairman of Highfield: 'Rugby league fans are a queer lot, and very insular. Widnes folk hate Warrington, Warrington hate Widnes, and Featherstone people would rather die than watch Castleford.'

Quinn: 'My main worry was whether we were selling ourselves too cheap. The game was virtually bankrupt, and when a business is bankrupt, a predator can come in and just pick it up. Merger was the last thing we wanted, but we had to consider it. I said that while everyone was in broad agreement in that room, the shit would hit the fan in a serious way once we returned to our clubs. I drove away from Huddersfield knowing that I had to be at my best for the next few weeks. There was still a lot to fight for.'

Concern was also expressed about the clubs excluded from the deal, and who would receive no financial benefit. Lindsay was mandated to ask for more money from News Corporation. At around 11 p.m., he left the meeting to telephone Chisholm. He returned with an extra £2 million to be shared among the non-Super League clubs. 'This meant a one-off payment of £100,000 each,' said Lindsay. 'Bearing in mind that some of these clubs had annual turnovers of £50,000 and most had serious debts, I knew this could be a lifesaver for them.'

The meeting broke up at around 2 a.m., and just before the close of business, a legal representative of News Corporation, who had been stationed in an adjoining room, fielded questions. 'I don't think many of us got much sleep that night,' said Lindsay.

The extraordinary general meeting had been scheduled later that morning at Central Park, the home of Wigan. All thirty-two professional clubs plus representatives from three who lost their league places two years previously, Blackpool, Chorley and Nottingham, were invited. The Second Division chairmen arrived ignorant of the meeting in Huddersfield the previous night. At 10 a.m., Walker, sitting next to Lindsay at the top table and facing rows of the club officials, commenced proceedings. 'Gentlemen, this is the most important day in the history of rugby league since the meeting in the George Hotel a hundred years ago,' he said. 'Since "Framing the Future", the game had made major progress in many areas such as cost control and minimum ground standards. The only issue that had not been addressed was the large number of clubs in a small geographical area. Outside the game, rugby league had never been viewed so highly and now was the chance to take it into a new dimension.'

Lindsay gave an outline of the deal, saying that it had been put together in just three days, the result of which was a three-page heads of agreement. He explained the dizzying sums involved, the suggested shape of the new Super League, the move to the summer, and the mergers that would have to take place. Plans had been modified in the light of discussions in Huddersfield. The Welsh team would take part in the remodelled First Division, which was to comprise the eleven existing clubs not given Super League places, and there would be no promotion or relegation for the first two seasons. There was a reiteration of the need for quick decisions and the clubs were told that a vote would be held after the discussion.

Steve Wagner, Featherstone Rovers chairman: 'I only learned about the meeting earlier that morning. I couldn't believe that I was being asked to vote on something that would radically alter the future of my club, and the game as a whole, with only three hours' notice. This was fast reality. We were told that if we left it twenty-four hours, the offer would no longer be on the table.'

Mike O'Neill, Keighley chairman: 'It was a bolt out of the blue for me, having not been at the Council meeting the previous Wednesday or at Huddersfield the night before. I had gone to Wigan in a relaxed frame of mind. We were about to win promotion and I was still on a high. That week, we had signed Daryl Powell [the Great Britain stand-off] for £130,000 and had already started selling tickets for the big games the following season. Now we were back where we started from. I was stunned and confused. It was like hearing of a death in the family. After the meeting, I drove a few miles out of Wigan and pulled into a lay-by. I just sat there trying to collect my thoughts, wondering how the club's supporters would take it.'

One of the most outspoken men at the meeting was the Widnes chairman, Jim Mills, a physically intimidating character who played prop forward for Widnes and Great Britain in the Seventies. He had been at the races at Aintree the previous day and had not been present at the meeting in Huddersfield when it had been decided that his club were to be first reserves for the Super League.

O'Neill: 'The one thing I remember clearly from the meeting was Jim Mills virtually stepping over me in his eagerness to put his point across. "Let me get at them," he said.' Mills made an impassioned speech about the traditions of his club and their record of success, which over the past two decades had been bettered only by Wigan. He received much support from the floor.

Mills: 'I played hell with them. A lot of them sat there with their mouths open. I couldn't believe we were expected to make decisions about the future of the game with such little notice. I felt that the negotiations were done much too quickly, and too few people were involved. There was a definite feeling that everything had to be done today, or the money would disappear tomorrow.' Mills reminded his colleagues that Widnes had been the league's second most successful club over the previous twenty years, and were about to embark on the construction of a new £6 million stadium.

Having listened to Mills's pleas, the chairman of Swinton, Malcolm White, proposed a merger between Warrington and Widnes, and that the club should be called Merseyside.

Malcolm White: 'I thought Jim had a reasonable grouse. After all, his club were already in the top division. The only way forward was for them to amalgamate with Warrington, even though Warrington were unhappy with that, saying that they wanted their own club.'

Mills: 'I accepted the principle, even though I couldn't see it working. There is such passion and rivalry between the fans. What common ground is there, for instance, between Hull and Hull KR? And they're in the same city. I felt the merger with Warrington was a non-starter, but at least we had our foot in the door.'

Walker told the meeting that it was regrettable that decisions had to be taken very quickly but the News Corporation offer was not going to be on the table indefinitely. 'If no agreement is reached today,' he explained, 'the money could be lost for ever. Time is not on our side.' Ironically, given the way events were soon to take over, he added that the deal 'would allow rugby league to retain control of its own destiny'.

Lindsay then read out a fax from Ken Arthurson in Australia which asked clubs to delay making a decision. This was viewed sceptically by those present, who believed that had the situation been reversed, the Australian clubs would not listen to pleadings from their British cousins.

Just after midday came the vote. This took the form of each club name being called alphabetically, and the respective representatives were invited to say yes or no. Barrow were first. Yes. Batley, about to win promotion from the Second Division, came next. 'Yes, reluctantly,' said Stephen Ball, their chairman. One by one, the answers came in the affirmative. Only Chorley, who abstained, went against the tide. At 12.15, the meeting was closed and Lindsay met the press in an adjoining room. 'This is not a hijack or a take-over,' he told them. 'It is a glorious opportunity which we have decided to accept.' He did not mention the sum of money involved. With that, everyone went home to watch the Grand National. Lindsay, however, went to Aintree where he was guest in the private box of Jonathan Martin, BBC's head of sport.

News of the Super League reverberated around the sporting world and stunned the rugby league community. The idea that some of the game's most famous clubs could submerge their own identity and amalgamate with their traditional rivals to form new, cosmetically engineered, 'superclubs' was, at best, fraught with logistical problems and, in the eyes of many, constituted a betrayal of the game's heritage. Nevertheless, there was an economic reality that, for almost all present, was a weightier issue. A spokesman for the rugby league supporters' association captured the schizophrenic mood. 'It could be the game's biggest opportunity to promote and develop itself,' said John Drake. 'But the club mergers are going to cause an absolute furore. There's going to be blood in the streets in Featherstone and Castleford.'

Peter Higham, Warrington director: 'I didn't vote to merge with Widnes, I voted for the £75 million. In the overall interests of the game, I had no choice.'

Joe Warham, Leeds director and council representative: 'The deal was manna from heaven. I had misgivings about the mergers and the demise of some famous names, but we had to throw off our insular shackles. I adapted John Donne: "No club is an island." In any case, some of them would have lost their identity when they disappeared into oblivion. We couldn't be held back by the question of local loyalties. Here was an opportunity for our beloved game to get worldwide exposure, and we had to grab it. I was excited by the prospect of spreading the game with franchises in major cities in Britain and Europe.'

Fletcher: 'I have said that ours is still a cloth cap and clogs game, and that we need to get our own house in order before we think about expanding. But I was accused of trying to stand in the way of progress.'

The unanimity of the vote at Wigan was not necessarily a reflection that this was a wholly good thing for the game. While most representatives agreed that the game's dire financial state needed root-and-branch treatment, and that this was a once-in-a lifetime offer that should not be rejected out of hand, there was a widespread belief among those present that voting against the plan would mean exclusion from further meetings. Supporters, meanwhile, felt they had been let down by their own chairmen, who had effectively voted them out of existence. But, as Mike O'Neill told Keighley's angry spectators during an on-the-field address the following day: 'I voted for the Super League because I want to fight it. But I can't fight it from the outside.' At Leeds, the chairman Alf Davies said that 'a gun was held to our heads' and that the clubs were told to 'vote in favour or you're out'.

The mood that afternoon at Keighley, a once-thriving mill town on the fringes of Brontë country and now a dormitory community for Bradford, six miles away, was understandably sour. On passing through the turnstiles, supporters were invited to sign a petition against the Super League, while others carried banners claiming that Lindsay was a traitor. At the end of the match, there was an orchestrated protest on the pitch, specially laid on for the television cameras. Yet rugby league folk tend to be stoics, and I overheard the following exposition in the queue for the gents: 'First game of next season, Toulouse away. Coaches leave the club on Thursday. Return by Wednesday morning.'

Keighley had reason to be upset. They had just secured promotion to the First Division for the first time in their history, the culmination of four years of dramatic progress which had seen the club transformed from one of the game's poorest relations, attracting crowds counted in hundreds rather than thousands, into a well-supported, successful club. This was achieved mainly through a far-sighted policy of selling the game to the local community, particularly in the schools. There were stunts that were held up to ridicule – in 1991, they changed their name to Keighley Cougars; their dishevelled ground, formerly Lawkholme Lane, became Cougar Park; they painted paw prints on the pavements leading to the ground, and had all manner of what could loosely be called pre-match entertainment. The scepticism that greeted Keighley's ambitious plans was rooted in the history of similar attempts to invest this intimate game with hints of what is crassly assumed to be 'glamour'.

Huddersfield had tried it in 1984. One of the league's founder members, the club had enjoyed a rich and successful history, but had become locked into a seemingly terminal decline. The directors thought cosmetic surgery was the answer, so they changed their name to Huddersfield Barracudas (a species that, as far as can be deduced, has no particular connection with the West Yorkshire mill town) and their famous Fartown ground, a symbol of the decaying state of the club, was renamed Arena 84. Given that Huddersfield supporters were alone, probably in the entire world of sport, in urging on their team not by its name but with cries of 'Come on, Fartown', the idea was fatuous in the extreme. They returned to being plain old Huddersfield three years later. As an example of how old ways die hard in rugby league, the club's nickname is still the Fartowners, even though they now play at the new McAlpine Stadium.

At Keighley, however, where there was no deeply ingrained tradition to overthrow and, with nothing to lose, the phoney Americanization worked. Young supporters – who were, after all, the main target audience – bought it, and their mums and dads followed. Success on the field was quickly reflected in higher crowds – in 1990, Keighley's average attendance was 936; by the end of the 94–95 season, when they won the Second Division championship, this was up to 3,723, not bad in a town with a population of 58,000. Gimmicks or not, this was held up as a model of how rugby league on a relatively small scale could be made to work. (And when you see a man in his eighties banging his walking stick in time with Queen's 'We will rock you' – the tedious accompaniment to every Keighley try – cynicism seems misplaced.) But now, as they stood at the threshold of the First Division, Keighley found the door slammed in their face. Their supporters were justified in wondering why a Super League was seen as an economic necessity. They believed that their example had demonstrated that the future lay in careful nourishment of the game at its roots, not in turning the structure upside down in pursuit of a mogul's millions.

O'Neill: 'We felt badly let down. We had been held up as an example to the rest of the league of how to revive the game in the community. Almost every club, including Wigan, visited us to see how we did it. Now they didn't want to know us.'

Elsewhere in the league, the Super League proposals attracted a fury that was engendered less by a feeling of rough justice than by the perfidy that had been dealt. Nowhere is the strength of the association between club and community so apparent as in Featherstone, the tiny Yorkshire mining town which has often been characterized as a set of traffic lights on the road between Leeds and Pontefract. In the not too distant past, residents used to attach their washing lines to the outer walls of the club's Post Office Road ground but, beyond these tangible connections, the rugby club provided the focal point of the town's activities and gave it a pride of its own, something that had been eroded by the decline of traditional industries. In towns such as Featherstone, where the two pits now stand idle, and Castleford, where the loss of their five pits was compounded by the closure of a major glassworks, rugby league is integral to the social fabric.

Wagner: 'After the meeting at Wigan, I had a gut feeling that the merger was a non-starter. Now that coalmining has gone, and there's no heavy industry here, Featherstone Rovers is the last remaining part of the town's tradition, a tradition that we are steeped in. I was sure the people would fight for it in the same way as they fought to keep the pits open. The only thing in Featherstone to warm the hearts of the people is Rovers. Our success down the years has put Featherstone on the map, and whatever the financial sense of a merger, the common view was that it would have been a disaster for the town.'

The thought that their club could be bought and sold as part of the furniture of a bigger deal was seen by the community as an act of deep treachery. Some years previously, Ian Clayton, a Featherstone man and local arts administrator wrote, with some prescience: 'What would Fev be without rugby, or Cas or Leigh, or anywhere? Small grey towns that had their day, that were born from coal and died with it, like so many in the north.' His sentiments were shared by thousands who cared and, in the spring of 1995, they took to the streets in Featherstone, propelled by the same tide of anger and rejection that had mobilized them during the miners' strike eleven years earlier. Their opposition to the Super League – the insult of losing their own club with its rich tradition was aggravated by being forced into bed with their deadliest rivals – was proudly paraded. Feelings also ran high in Castleford and Wakefield, and in Warrington and Widnes, and indeed at all points where merger was on the agenda.

Wagner: 'It was a time of my life that I would not like to live through again. I received threatening phone calls, and I was verbally abused in the street, told I was a Judas and that I was selling the club down the river. There was even a banner at the ground that read "Murdoch, Lindsay, Wagner – OUT". I thought, crikey, I don't deserve to be put in that bracket. I'm about £50 billion behind Murdoch.'

In Hull, where the renaissance in the early Eighties had seen five-figure crowds at both clubs and a host of trophies brought back to the city, the mood was equally defiant. Len Casey, one of a rare breed who has played for both Hull clubs, said that the thought that a century of sporting rivalry should be cast aside 'went down like a loaded gun'. John Godber, the local playwright, added: 'Who do they think they're kidding with these new names like Calder and Humber? They sound like characters from *Gladiators*.' On a wall near the entrance to Hull KR's Craven Park, the graffiti made the supporters' feelings clear: 'No merger. East Hull keep Rovers. Ask the fans now!'

Even though most of the chairmen involved agreed that mergers involved possibly intractable problems, meetings were held in an effort to bring about a solution.

Quinn: 'I met John Wilkinson, the Salford chairman, at a hotel in Cheshire. We had a pleasant meal and spent four hours discussing merger proposals. We couldn't agree on a thing. He believed he had the best coach in the game, I believed I did, and so it went on. We found no common ground. So we decided to go our own ways and see what happened. From the start, I don't think enough consideration was given to the history and culture of our game. Australia is a big, wild place, but there is an intimacy about rugby league in Britain.' Later, Wilkinson, an urbane man, told a meeting of chairmen that there could indeed be a merger between Salford and Oldham, 'only if we play in Oldham, Jim Quinn is the chairman, and Andy Goodway [the Oldham coach] becomes the coach'.

Stuart Farrar, chairman of Wakefield Trinity: 'Nobody

wanted to see our name, one of the most famous in the league, disappear. But after the initial shock, I began to recognize the reality. There is a population of 250,000 in the Wakefield Metropolitan area supporting three clubs; Leeds has a population of a million with one major club. Without the hindrance of local rivalries in Wakefield, Castleford and Featherstone, we had a chance to broaden the supporter base and attract new people to the game. A merger of the three was the answer.'

Wakefield's financial problems were acute, gates were poor and several of their best players had been attracted by other teams. The club's shareholders voted to back the merger plans.

Farrar: 'After the last game of the season, I went into the dressing room to talk to the players. At the time, I believed it was the end of the line for Wakefield Trinity. I started to thank them for everything they had done, but I just broke down. Some of the players, particularly those who had been around for many years, were also in tears. It was a very emotional time.'

The revolution of a century earlier, forcing the schism between league and union, had been led by forces from the inside; the distaste with which many within the game viewed the events of the spring of 1995 was informed by a feeling that these changes were to be imposed by an outside agency, and one who has shown little interest in, and no empathy with, rugby league. There were peaceful demonstrations at many grounds, especially at the Easter Bank Holiday Derby matches, when fans believed they were seeing the end of traditional rivalries. It was not just a case of vocal protests, banners and graffiti. The cause was taken up in the House of Commons, the emotive issues were given wide coverage in the national media, there were threats of legal action, particularly from Keighley, and accusations of betrayal from the Australian Rugby League, who had been fighting a battle against Murdoch's establishment of his breakaway Star League down under. The all-party Parliamentary rugby league group, led by David Hinchliffe MP, expressed concern about rugby league being sold 'lock, stock and barrel to a private media interest' during a ninety-minute debate in the Commons while the Labour Party were keen to see the deal referred to the Monopolies and Mergers Commission. It soon became clear that the proposed mergers were not going to be forced through and, by the end of April, two weeks after the groundbreaking meeting at Wigan, there was the chance that the whole episode would turn into a public relations disaster.

David Howes, chief executive of St Helens and the league's former public relations officer: 'There was little consideration given to how the news should be broken to supporters. It was a sensitive issue and should have been handled delicately. The principle of merger was worthy of rational debate, but instead people thought they were being told: "By the way, the club you've supported for thirty years is dead." The approach should have been more like: "We know you like your corner shop, but the supermarket will be better," and not "Don't go to the corner shop – it's shut."'

Wagner: 'People power won the day. We are a club run by our members and when we balloted them, they voted overwhelmingly to go it alone.'

Jim Quinn: 'In all the furore surrounding the mergers, the culture of rugby league shone through. In the main, it is a game built by, played by and watched by working-class people. They may not have very much in their lives. But what they have, they treasure.'

Six months earlier, the 'Framing the Future' document had concluded: 'If there was one lasting impression of the work in rugby league, it is of everyone feeling passionate about the game and its development. Also of resentment of its parochial and minority sport image.' But when it came to the big question, the reality was somewhat different. Passion could not be separated from parochialism; supporters wanted the game to stay close to its roots, and they certainly didn't want their sense of identity to be sacrificed on the altar of financial imperative and marketing initiative.

The views at Featherstone were reflected elsewhere. Castleford's shareholders also voted against the plans, although Wakefield expressed a keenness to explore the possibility of merging with someone else; Carlisle, Barrow and Whitehaven rejected the formation of a Cumbrian club with Workington Town, who were allowed to pursue a Super League place on their own; Oldham and Salford failed to agree on anything; the amalgamation of Widnes and Warrington was called off as both were given entry to the Super League when Toulouse pulled out; even the merger between Hull and Hull KR, widely regarded as the one which made the most geographical and economic sense, came to nothing, although discussions continued.

Lindsay: 'The emotional issues took over from an objective discussion of the changes. With the name Rupert Murdoch attached to the end of the offer, it brought up images in people's minds of Wapping and the miners' strike, and everything they felt they had been battling against. It was fuelled by MPs, who were making statements that brought a lot of passion into the issue. For about three weeks, the emotional argument swept a pocket of Yorkshire. It didn't sweep Lancashire. There were no marches in Oldham or Salford, or in Warrington. Yet amid all this furore, the chairman of Featherstone was saying: "We're going bust, we can't pay the bills." But his was a weak voice lost in the wind. No one was listening. And the sensible discussion that could and should have taken place, with forums of supporters, never happened. It was all inflamed by our absolute need to make an urgent decision. It was still unclear what was happening in Australia. Nobody knew what was going on there, not even Ken Arthurson or Kerry Packer. There were so many vested interests, and nobody knew who the players were going to sign for. We couldn't take the chance of losing the deal. If it had collapsed, I think the will to survive among club chairmen would have been weakened so much that it might have broken the back of rugby league. If they had seen £1 million a year pass through their fingers after years of stoic resistance to the banks and creditors, it would have killed off their spirit. That would have been unforgivable. We had to put some coal in the engine.'

Meanwhile, back at Sky headquarters, Chisholm had become concerned about the adverse publicity the deal was attracting. On Monday, 24 April, he met Lindsay in London. Lindsay explained that because of the depth of feeling among supporters and the difficulties the clubs were experiencing in bringing about mergers, he was unable to deliver a reality based on the motion passed at Wigan. Chisholm said that he was disappointed with the reaction to his company's offer which, he said, 'was made in good faith and was very generous'. Lindsay explained that he and Walker had put together a revised set of proposals, which he was sure the clubs would accept at a meeting scheduled for the following Sunday, the day after the Challenge Cup Final. With the promise that the turbulence would be over, and that News Corporation would have their prize, Lindsay asked for another £10 million. Chisholm agreed to think about it and Lindsay returned to his London hotel. 'I couldn't sleep, I couldn't work through it, I couldn't do anything,' recalled Lindsay. The following morning, Chisholm called. 'I've been thinking about the £10 million,' he said. 'The answer's no.' 'Shit,' said Lindsay. He hadn't allowed for Chisholm's cruel sense of humour. 'Only kidding,' he said. 'You've got your money. But that's got to be the end of it.'

On the morning of 30 April, at the end of the most bewildering month in the sport's history, the chairmen were called back to the Hilton Hotel in Huddersfield. After nearly six hours of animated discussion, which took place without Keighley (who were in another room in the hotel with their legal advisers), all the mergers were shelved and a format not that dissimilar to the one already in place was revealed to the world. The Super League would include the teams who had finished in the top ten places in the First Division, plus London and Paris. There was to be a First Division of eleven teams and a Second Division of ten, also based on league finishing positions. The News Corporation financial package was raised to £87 million over the five-year contract period: Super League clubs would receive £900,000 a season, First Division clubs would get between £200,000 and £700,000 depending on league positions, and Second Division clubs would get a minimum of £100,000 and a maximum of £135,000 based on criteria relating to off-the-field initiatives. For the first season, clubs could spend the money how they saw fit, but from the second year, there would be guidelines for spending in line with the recommendations of 'Framing the Future'. Promotion would be on a one-up, one-down basis between the Super League and Division One, and it would be two-up, two-down between Divisions One and Two.

Despite repeated attempts to persuade Keighley to enter into the debate, they refused to join the meeting. Only Widnes, who had ridden an emotional switchback – first excluded, then told to merge, then included, and finally, because of their league position, left out again – voted against the new plan and resolved to institute a legal action of their own. They were told that the extra £10 million from News Corporation was contingent on the condition that there would be no litigation. Jim Mills, the Widnes chairman, then raised the temperature of the meeting by suggesting that 'some people had been less than 100 per cent truthful'. Rodney Walker's reaction was furious. In a passionate defence of Lindsay, he said that the chief executive had suffered personally because of allegations made in the Press, in the House of Commons and by some of the clubs. He invited anyone who did not trust the league's board of directors to speak up or leave the meeting. Kevan Gorge, the Workington chairman and a member of the board added: 'I have never witnessed anything as infantile as the way some clubs are behaving. News Corporation must think they are dealing with a crowd of idiots.'

Lindsay himself took up the theme. 'I have been angered to the point of dismay by the actions of certain clubs,' he announced. 'I am particularly infuriated by certain people new to the game who have indirectly questioned my integrity. The topical term used in modern times is the word "bung". I have received no bung.' He admitted that he was an ambitious man and that he would be delighted to assume a role as head of a World Super League if it became available. 'I see nothing wrong in cherishing that ambition,' he concluded. Walker added: 'I too can assure the clubs that Mr Lindsay has not received one penny for all his hard work.'

There were other unhappy parties. The league's five-man board had clearly invested much in the merger plans and the expansion into new areas, while others felt that the revised scheme was a compromise too far.

Stuart Farrar: 'I never believed that the Super League should just be a reincarnated First Division. Murdoch's money isn't just to keep clubs alive; it is supposed to regenerate rugby league and to prepare us for the next fifty years.'

Eddie Ashton: 'The decision to merge Castleford, Featherstone and Wakefield may well have been the right one. It is hard to see the game ever dying in this area, because we breed players here, but the worsening economic climate has meant that all our crowds are getting smaller and smaller. And even with the Murdoch money, we will still be competing against each other for players, and that's an expensive business.'

Joe Warham: 'I feel we pussyfooted into the Super League. We had a chance to create a truly national sport but because of the outcry of a few thousand – and that's all they were – the dream was eroded and the money was spread more widely.

It's not a question of the poor getting poorer, the poor are getting richer on the backs of the rich. I can understand local devotion, but we have been forced to limit our horizons.'

Jack Robinson, the Wigan chairman, also expressed his disappointment that the mergers had not been effected. 'We were looking forward to a more competitive league,' he said.

While some clearly felt that a reluctance to shake off the parochialism of the past had hindered progress towards a brave new world, the revised plan ensured that there was a greater degree of unity in the game. Keighley called off their legal action, Widnes suffered a costly defeat in theirs, and the sport was reconstituted to begin its new life in Paris on 29 March 1996. Many questions remained unanswered, but at least the betrothal to Murdoch had not riven rugby league in Britain as it had done in Australia.

It proved to be a marriage made not in heaven or hell, but somewhere in between. Like Huddersfield.

SIX

BOOKMAKER AND ARCHITECT

Maurice Lindsay, the man who made the deal

At the height of the debate over some of the more controversial proposals of the Super League deal, there was a joke doing the rounds in rugby league country. It went like this. Saddam Hussein looks in his mirror every morning and asks: 'Mirror, mirror on the wall, who is the most hated man of all?' Without fail, the mirror answers: 'You are, Oh mighty President.' One day, he asks the question and fails to get the customary response. Angrily, he turns to his aides and asks: 'Who is this Maurice Lindsay?'

For the three weeks or so between the first draft of the Super League and the final agreement which consigned to history (for the time being at least) the question of enforced mergers of clubs, Lindsay, chief executive of the rugby league, took on demonic proportions for a sizeable proportion of the game's followers. They believed he had shepherded the agreement through with unseemly haste, had little regard for the traditions of the game or the sensitivity of supporters and had sold their birthright to a man who was interested only in his own gain. That, of course, was the simplistic view, but so high did passions run at that time – probably the most turbulent period in the game's history – that this was by no means an uncommon view. Lindsay was applauded by most club chairmen, having negotiated a deal that would save them from the abyss into which they felt they were heading. In private, they told him that he had pulled off a masterstroke; in public, faced with the vitriolic response of their supporters, their support became more equivocal. So it seemed that Lindsay, hitherto widely respected as an administrator both inside and outside the game, could be excused for feeling that he was virtually friendless.

At some grounds, especially at those where merger was on the agenda, banners proclaimed he was a latter-day Judas, he was subject to hate mail after a fly poster printed his address and urged malcontents to make their feelings known, and was, it seemed, accosted by disgruntled fans almost every time he set foot outside his bunker in Leeds. In Widnes, where they were particularly upset at their club's treatment, a hurtful leaflet was distributed. Under photographs of Lindsay and Rupert Murdoch, the following was printed: 'What you have to remember is that these two jolly bedfellows are businessmen and as such are only interested in making money. The game we watch from the terraces is of secondary importance.'

However, the nadir for Lindsay came on Cup Final day at Wembley on Saturday, 29 April 1995. The Wigan team whose rise he had orchestrated had just beaten Leeds to win their eighth successive Challenge Cup. On his way out of the stadium, he exchanged pleasantries with the jubilant Wigan fans before returning, with his girlfriend, to his Jaguar (registration number, M1 RFL). Lindsay inched his way out of the car park, and then stopped at a zebra crossing. A middle-aged man, his wife and their son were crossing, man and boy wearing Castleford shirts. The man stopped halfway across, noticed Lindsay in the driver's seat and simply stood there unleashing a volley of abuse. It was ugly enough to stop the traffic on the pavements, never mind the road. He continued to shout at Lindsay for several minutes, before his wife shook him and pleaded with him to stop. 'It was extremely upsetting and embarrassing,' recalls Lindsay. 'It wasn't just the language he was using in front of the child, it was also the way he was brandishing his son and asking repeatedly: "Why are you ruining his future?" I could see how genuinely upset he was, but there was no reasoning with him. I couldn't explain that what I was trying to do was consolidate his son's future. Like it or not, rugby league was going. A lot of people didn't want to admit it, but it was. Something had to happen.' Lindsay was eventually allowed to drive on, which he did in stunned silence. 'What also upset me about the incident was that I felt I hadn't got my argument across to the fans,' Lindsay explained. 'When they carried banners saying "Lindsay is a wanker" and they couldn't spell either Lindsay or wanker, that didn't worry me. But the image of that man on the zebra crossing stuck with me, largely because of his little boy. The incident left me in no doubt that there were too many people who were confused, who didn't understand. There were too many people who thought the News Corporation deal was the death knell for rugby league. They thought that I had engineered the whole thing, when in fact all I had done is brought back all these good tidings.'

The next day, at a hotel in Huddersfield, the final shape of the Super League was agreed upon by club chairmen and the retreat was beaten from many of the original proposals that had aroused such terrible anger in so many quarters of the game.

There were several occasions during those stormy weeks, says Paul Harrison, media manager at league headquarters, when Lindsay, after a wearying day, would wonder aloud, and usually rhetorically, whether it was worth all the effort. 'Maurice clearly relished the fight,' Harrison explains, 'but when it got so personal and so bitter, and it hammered him so much, I think he found it hard not to let it affect him. He could shrug off 95 per cent of it, whereas most people would only shrug off 50 per cent. But then it gets to you. And when he reached the point when he questioned whether it was worth it, my answer was always the same: "Maurice, you're a fighter, and don't let the bastards beat you."'

Ten months later, Lindsay showed no visible scars from the struggles he endured bringing the Super League to fruition. As the snow swirled outside, we sat beside the coal-effect fire in his spacious office at the new league headquarters on the outskirts of Leeds and Lindsay quoted Benjamin Disraeli's rebuke to those who opposed and jeered him: 'You are not listening to me. The day will come when you will have to listen to me.' The chief executive of the rugby league says he gained much strength from recalling that sentiment in recent times. He talks passionately about the historical figures with whom he most identified. 'I admire anyone who has stood firm in the face of injustice,' he says. 'I like leaders in every walk of life. I loved it when Martin Luther King was ramming home his points about the injustices of the system. I admire Jewish people, who have been oppressed down the years, but have stood firm, and that's why they are how they are. They're stubborn, and they'll argue with you, but that comes from centuries of being oppressed.' In his business life, Lindsay is more free-market economist than freedom fighter, yet even his critics will admit that one of his guiding principles as an administrator is to achieve what he believes is a just deal for the game he loves. There are those who feel that Lindsay is on a personal mission, his single-mindedness rooted in a desire to go down in history. Clearly, there is an ego at work, but, while some question his methods, it is difficult to challenge his motives. Lindsay is vehement in his rejection of rumours that he received payments from the Murdoch organization as a reward for delivering the Super League deal, and there is no evidence that this suggestion is any more than part of a malicious whispering campaign.

Lindsay was fifty-four years old when the Super League kicked off and seems an unlikely choice for the role of demon.

He is a small man (no more than 5ft 6in), veers towards portliness, and has the bustling gait of someone perpetually in a hurry. His features suggest amiability, and he has the jowliness of a kindly uncle. When he speaks, he does so deliberately and softly, with a singsong intonation that is at odds with the macho image of his sport. His speech brings to mind the Bradford-born artist David Hockney, or a character played by Alan Bennett. But neither his stature nor his manner has been any impediment to Lindsay's ability to make a mark in a world dominated by men of more obviously commanding physique. He has emerged as a dominant presence, and his writ in world rugby league now runs large. Maurice Lindsay, former bookmaker, the man who rejuvenated Wigan, and architect of the Super League, is a force in the land.

It was wartime London, and Ann Lindsay was pregnant with her first child when the air raid siren sounded. Mrs Lindsay and her husband Nicholas left their small terraced house in Shoreditch in the East End and went to the tube station which acted as an underground shelter. Several hours passed before the all-clear was signalled, but when the Lindsays returned home, they found a pile of rubble where their house used to stand. Ann Lindsay, the daughter of a farmer from the west coast of Ireland, had come over to England with her husband, an ambitious tailor, in search of work. Nicholas Lindsay got a job with the Admiralty, who employed him to make uniforms, and the couple had scraped together enough to buy their Shoreditch home. Now their dream of a prosperous future in London lay in ruins. The Lindsays acted decisively; Ann went to join her sister, who was living in Lancashire, while Nicholas, foreseeing the difficulties of finding work there, joined the army. Several months later, on 8 May 1941, Ann gave birth to a son, Maurice Patrick, who was to be the couple's only child.

After the war, during which he fought in Burma, Nicholas returned to join his wife and son at his sister-in-law's home in Horwich, a railway engineering town midway between Bolton and Wigan. He quickly got a job as a tailor, working for a company in Bolton, and earned the decent sum of £6 a week. With that, he was able to rent a small house (which he eventually bought) and send Maurice to Thornleigh Salesian College, a distinguished direct grant grammar school in Bolton. At Thornleigh, there was a sizeable pupil population from Wigan, where they had no Roman Catholic grammar school. Most of them were rugby league supporters, and it was here that the young Maurice, whose sporting interests at that time revolved around soccer and cross-country, was first introduced to the game that was to shape his life.

'Up until the age of twelve, I had never seen a rugby league match,' he explains, 'but the lads at the school were fanatical about it.' Curious, Maurice went to a game at Central Park, the home of Wigan, on his own. 'I wanted to see it for myself,' he says. It was 1953, he was twelve years old, and Maurice took the No 16 bus from Horwich to see Wigan play the redoubtable Oldham team of that period. 'It was in the days when the home team changed their colours if they clashed. So Oldham played in their own cherry-and-white hoops. And they hammered Wigan. I was bemused that the famous cherry-and-whites I had gone to see got slaughtered by a team wearing the same colours.' That first experience left a deep impression on Lindsay, and probably informed much of his later professional life. 'There was a big crowd there, and I stood at the corner. I have a vivid memory – I can see him now – of a spiv standing at that same corner. Five minutes before the game started, he shouted: "Anyone want to back Wigan? They're asking for a start in Oldham, but I'll back Oldham level against Wigan." All the local diehards who were around him jumped in and bet anything from a half-crown to ten shillings, a pretty big sum in those days. The

Oldham man, who obviously knew his rugby, cleaned up.' Even at twelve, Lindsay, who later became a successful bookmaker himself, realized that, with a little nerve and a lot of nous, there are enjoyable ways to make money.

As for the match itself, Lindsay recalls the variety of the game. 'I can picture these fantastically strong, brave athletes crashing down the field. I was impressed also that they were all different shapes and sizes. I had been used to watching soccer at Bolton where the inside forward always had Brylcreemed hair, and the centre forward had a big head, and the full-backs had knobbly knees and the goalkeeper was always fat.' Lindsay admits that he was fascinated by the game of rugby league, but he certainly was not hooked. He returned to school, took the mickey out of the Wigan fans among his schoolmates and continued to follow Bolton Wanderers, where Nat Lofthouse was in his pomp. It was a year or so later that he was persuaded to make a return trip to Central Park. 'All my mates were talking about Billy Boston, this new black flash that Wigan had signed,' he said. 'They were bragging about him and I thought I had better go to see him for myself. And I watched him go down the wing, and he used to knock people off with his hip. When I saw Billy Boston play, that was it really. I was hooked.' There were other Wigan players of that time who fed Lindsay's imagination. 'Alex Murphy burst on the scene as a sixteen-year-old soon afterwards,' he explains. 'He was lightning around the scrum. I'll never forget that.' By now, Lindsay had been accepted as a member of the Wigan gang, and went to every home match. When they were playing away, he went to Bolton.

The only interruption to this pattern came from Lindsay's pursuit of personal sporting goals. He became a member of Horwich Railwaymen's Institute Harriers and took part in club cross-country meetings all over the north of England. In the summer months, he sprinted, and once won the British Rail Invitation sprint in London. He was also a talented schoolboy boxer, and was unbeaten in the 8-stone category for almost five years, defeating the Northern ABA champion and the Lancashire Schoolboys champion along the way. The realization that he did not have a serious future in boxing came to Lindsay, painfully, one night at Chorley Town Hall when he was seventeen. 'I was fighting a lad called Collinson from Chorley,' he recalls, 'and he battered me. He really did. I fought him again, and he was too good for me then as well. I knew then that I was never going to be world class if I couldn't beat guys like him. So I concentrated on other things, like women and drinking.' While Lindsay was certainly above the waterline as far as academic achievement was concerned, he was no a model scholar. 'I passed my O Levels and couldn't get out of school quick enough,' he says. 'I wouldn't have stayed on if you had given me £1,000 a week.' Lindsay left school and signed up for a British Rail accountancy apprentice scheme. It was a four-year-term and Lindsay was able to work in his home town, in the shadow of the Horwich locomotive works. He completed his apprenticeship, and stayed on for an extra year, but never felt that this was likely to be a lifetime's career. 'My mother always wanted me to be an accountant,' he says. 'She thought it was a respectable occupation. She wanted me to work in an office. She had come from a farm in Ireland and my father was a simple tailor, so she just wanted me to have what she considered respectability. The pillars of local society then were the local doctor, the local headmaster or people who had positions of seniority in offices. I was a slow developer,' Lindsay admits, 'and I didn't really work things out for myself until I was in my twenties. So I just went along with what my mother and father said, and I didn't put up much of a fight.'

Parental influence was clearly very strong and Lindsay tells how he went, with a friend, to take an examination at the Central Electricity Generating Board. It transpired that Lindsay was offered a job, but when the letter arrived at the family home at 7, Webb Street, his mother confiscated it, believing the job was not right for her son. 'I remember looking in the cupboard about a year later and finding the letter,' Lindsay explains. 'It said that I had top marks in the exam and they were offering me a position in Wigan. She'd hidden the bloody thing so I hadn't even replied. Who knows where I would have ended up? At that stage in my life, I didn't really have a clue what I wanted, and I didn't really care, either. I used to be out with the lads, having a good time, knocking off the birds, just enjoying myself.'

At twenty-one years old, Lindsay began to realize that accountancy was not the career for him. He wanted to move into industry, and joined Vibroplant, a local plant hire company. It proved to be the last time Lindsay would be in someone else's employ. Within seven years, he had risen to become the company's general manager. 'Even so, my real desire was to work for myself,' he says. In 1970, together with two senior colleagues, Lindsay left to form his own plant hire company, Lee Lindsay Ltd. After eighteen months, he sold out to his two partners and formed the Lindsay Group, a conglomeration of companies dealing in plant hire and site accommodation. Much of his trade resulted from rebuilding work in Northern Ireland and he prospered into the Eighties, when Lindsay sold out again. He now has a considerable personal fortune to call upon.

The only other line of business that attracted Lindsay was bookmaking. Lindsay had been taken to the Cheltenham Festival as a child by his father, and developed a great love of National Hunt racing, which he puts second to rugby league in his list of sporting passions. 'At Cheltenham, my dad used to drink Guinness all day and do his money in and I went along for the ride. Racing has always been a hobby of mine. The crack on the racecourse is first class. Most of them like a drink – as I do – and there is a real sense of fun,' he explains. In 1974, 'just to fill in the evenings', Lindsay developed another company, Lindsay Leisure, which dealt in football coupons and took bets on horse racing. 'That provided me with considerable spending money. I enjoyed the hard work, but it was the excitement of racing that was was the most attractive thing.' Lindsay would sometimes dash from meetings at his plant hire company and, an hour or so later, was to be seen taking bets on the rails at northern racetracks, a milieu in which he felt comfortable. Through his first-hand experience, Lindsay gives bookies the sort of standing that most of us would reserve for those in other vocations, nurses or teachers for instance. 'Bookmaking is an honourable profession,' he says. 'I find racecourse bookmakers very honest: they have to settle on the spot, and even disputes are settled very honourably. Every transaction they strike – and they are striking one every second – their integrity has to be absolutely unquestioned, and it is. They are not my favourite people, some of them, but it's one of the most reputable businesses in this country, if not the most, because people in the City are not as straight. So I defend them.'

Bookmaking gave Lindsay the opportunity to get close to National Hunt racing, which he believes shares a number of attributes with rugby league. 'If any two sportsmen are alike,' says Lindsay, 'it's the National Hunt jockey and the rugby league player. Both get smashed to pieces, both enjoy the wit and humour in the changing room, both put their body on the line every time they go out to play, and for years neither of them got true financial reward. They are also uncomplaining. You rarely hear Adrian Maguire [a leading jump jockey] or Kelvin Skerrett [legendary prop forward] whingeing. They get smashed jaws, they get pain, but they rarely complain.' Lindsay, now with the resources, has indulged his passion for racing by owning horses and has a third-share, along with two other senior figures in rugby league, in a hurdler called Barrister's Boy.

He is clearly a man with a deep sense of purpose, and has

a legendary appetite for work. But he has a respect bordering on envy for those able to adopt a more easygoing approach to life, and is particularly lyrical when talking of the Irish. Lindsay has a newly built detached house in Wigan and, during the week, lives in a house he has bought in a village near Leeds. He knows on which side of the Pennines he feels more comfortable. 'I prefer the environment in Lancashire because I find the people a very relaxed, carefree mob. This is because of the mixed nature of all the people in Lancashire with the Scousers and the Mancunians and the Wiganers. They're all different. There's a great mixture of influences. In Yorkshire, people have greater riches because the county is quite magnificent. But they have a very similar outlook on life to each other. Security is very important to them, and status too. Status is not important to a Scouser, or a Wiganer. They just like to eat, drink and be merry.' Lindsay has something of a reputation himself as a bon viveur, but finds that his work leaves little time for hedonistic pursuit. He sleeps very little, maybe three or four hours a night, and is invariably awake to watch the 5 a.m. news bulletin on Sky. 'I envy people who can live life for the moment. I have promised myself that it's something I shall work towards – not to achieve the financial platform, because I had that some time ago, but working towards a position where you're prepared to bloody do it. And I must be a different animal because I actually enjoy the buzz, the hype and the pressure.'

Work is the drug for Lindsay, and his non-stop schedule – personal calls from anywhere in the world can be put through instantly to his car or mobile phone, he told me proudly – gives him little time for self-analysis. I asked him when he first recognized in himself the restless determination to succeed. 'I don't think I can point to a specific period in my life,' he replied. 'You are just like that or you are not. I think I've always been like that. I've always been competitive and I've wanted to do well. I don't think it came from my mother and I don't think it came from my father. I don't analyse myself too much, but I do know that I am very determined.' So what would he like his epitaph to read? Lindsay thought for a few moments. 'He did have a go,' was his answer.

Rising to a challenge, Lindsay says, is what gives him the biggest satisfaction in his working life. 'There are some people, and I'm definitely one of them, who enjoy solving problems. When it can't be done, they love to find a way round it. I'm like that.' Some of those who have worked at close quarters with Lindsay point to his considerable mental agility. Paul Harrison, rugby league's media manager, admits to being left open-mouthed by Lindsay's powers of thinking on his feet. 'He's also got an incredible eye for detail,' says Harrison. 'Maurice will have a hundred conversations a day with various people, but he'll remember exactly what he said to you a week last Tuesday.'

Others who have worked closely with Lindsay have a different tale to tell. Harry Gration, a BBC sports reporter, was appointed as the league's public relations executive in February, 1994. 'Maurice's style of management is all-consuming,' he said. 'He is not very conversant with the art of delegation. When he arrived at rugby league headquarters in 1992, he was determined to impose the principles of business. He was meticulous about the accountancy, and liked to know where every penny was being spent. He was a tough manager, and was always on you, always wanting to know where you where and what you were doing. In the end, I found it completely exasperating.' Gration lasted almost exactly a year in the job, but left with no personal animosity for Lindsay. 'Maurice is a very proud, strong-willed character. and is a hard negotiator. I am certain that Rupert Murdoch was given a pretty good run for his money.'

Gration believes that Lindsay's determination to succeed as a world force in rugby league was fuelled by an incident at an international board meeting. 'There was some discussion concerning overseas development,' he explains, 'and Ken Arthurson [chairman of the Australian Board, and at that time all-powerful in the game] put down Maurice in a very patronizing way. It was as if he had slapped his wrists and told him not be such a naughty boy. I sensed then that Maurice resolved this would not happen to him again, and that if he got a chance to turn the tables, he would enjoy it to the full. The Aussies had made the mistake of underestimating Maurice. You underestimate him at your peril. He enjoys walking the tightrope.'

By his own admission, Lindsay is a perfectionist, and expects the same standards in those around him. 'He would always want you in at 8.15 in the morning, no matter how many hours you had put in that week, or whether you had been working the previous night,' says Gration. 'No one works harder than Maurice, however. I don't know what drives him on. I suppose it's a mixture of insecurity and will.' Lindsay himself believes that being worrisome is a quality. 'I am anxious about getting things right, but my first accountant told me never to worry about worrying. That's what makes a good businessman.'

Lindsay, according to Gration, inspires fear and loyalty in roughly equal measure among his colleagues and, while he has many acquaintances, he has relatively few friends. 'He's not an easy man to get to know,' says Gration, 'although that may be simply a function of the fact that he was the boss and felt he had to keep his distance. For about two weeks, around the death of his mother in the summer of 1994, I felt that I was getting close to him. I felt I was seeing the side of Maurice that I wanted to see. He had always seemed to shun socializing, but now he opened up.' Gration was one of the few mourners at the funeral of Ann Lindsay in Horwich, and remembers it as a genuinely warm occasion. 'Her death was clearly a profound moment in Maurice's life. She was a very significant figure for him. Her passing seemed to give him even greater will to succeed.' Ann Lindsay was buried in the town where she had arrived, by the force of necessity, some fifty-three years earlier. Her only child, the little boy who grew up to be a big man in his own world, stood at the graveside. He thought of the time when he was wealthy enough to send his parents on a cruise on the *Oriana* and his proud mother returned home with the menus from every meal on board. Maurice Lindsay could be certain of one thing: he had fulfilled, and then exceeded, his parents' expectations of him.

It seems incredible now, but there was a time, in the not too distant past, when Wigan did not look down imperiously on the rest of rugby league. In fact, when the decision was made to split the league into two divisions in 1973, the First Division was to be made up of the top sixteen teams in the league from the previous season and Wigan scraped in, having finished in sixteenth spot, and then only on points average. They just escaped relegation that season, but the following year finished in the runners-up position behind St Helens. But the decade ended badly, and in the 1979–80 season they suffered the ignominy of dropping through the trapdoor into the Second Division. A once-great club, with a Test match ground and the potential to attract huge crowds, they epitomized that soubriquet favoured by sports commentators – the sleeping giant. Maurice Lindsay, however, was very much awake. A successful local businessman with plenty of money to spare, Lindsay was well known at Central Park, having sponsored several games through his company. He had a shirt sponsorship deal with the successful local amateur club, Wigan St Patrick's, between 1976 and 1978, and claims to have been the first commercial backer of the amateur game. 'I progressed to sponsor matches at Wigan, but it was small-scale stuff, putting a few quid in for man-of-the-match, making a speech, and having a few drinks in the boardroom.

They knew I understood the game, and was friends with great former players like Alex Murphy and Jackie Edwards.

'At the time, I never dreamt of being on the board,' recalls Lindsay. 'But I did think that if I was in charge, I'd change this, or improve that, On the occasions when I went into the boardroom, I felt that the board were very good at dispensing whisky, but they didn't seem to have a common purpose. Wigan had a big board, with several different factions; in fact, they used to sit in different corners of the room after a match. And the players were kept below stairs in what was called the tea-room. There, the floor was covered in oil cloth and it was really cheap and nasty. There were cups of tea in the corner, while up in the boardroom they were drinking as much whisky as they wanted, and were pouring it with great largesse.'

As an informed outsider, it niggled away at Lindsay that affairs were not being conducted at his chosen club in the manner he thought best. 'The soul of the club wanted putting right,' he said. 'Even the supporters were regarded as being fortunate to be able to watch the team. Everything was wrong. It did cross my mind a couple of times that I would love to have a crack at this, but I was very occupied in business so I never dwelt on it.' The opportunity came looking for Lindsay. He arrived late for work one morning in 1979, and found the Wigan chairman, Harry Gostelow, pacing up and down outside his site office. He had come to invite Lindsay to join the board. The club had just sacked two directors and the case for Lindsay was made vociferously by Ken Broome, a former chairman and a major presence within the club. 'Within a week, I had been made vice-chairman and they put me in charge of the finances,' recalls Lindsay. 'The first thing I did was telephone one of the sacked directors, who was a chartered accountant, to answer some queries. I remember him saying to me: "Maurice, you'll never make it go at Wigan. The board's wrong, the town's wrong, the whole thing has gone." I never embarrassed him with that any time later, but I knew for years that he was embittered. As for the other sacked director, he was very suspicious of me but after five years of keeping his distance, he came up to me one day, shook my hand and said, "I just want to say it's been fantastic." That meant a lot to me.'

When Lindsay joined the Wigan board, there were nine other directors, so there was limited scope for the new man to make his presence felt immediately. His first ambition was to streamline the board. 'Wigan were being outstripped by other clubs, like Widnes, Hull, and Hull KR. I was friendly at the time with Ossie Davies [then chairman of Warrington] and they had a small board of directors who, together with the coach Alex Murphy, were making instant decisions, buying good players, and having a good deal of success. At Wigan, we were meeting from six in the evening until midnight and achieving bugger all. We weren't getting anywhere, there was no single plan that we could all agree on, and the factions were still there. We had to have a new management structure. And that meant a small board. I knew that was the way forward.' As Lindsay took his place in the Wigan boardroom, the other vacant seat was taken by Jack Robinson, who went on to become chairman of the club. Lindsay saw in Robinson a fellow believer. 'We were like-minded in many respects,' explained Lindsay. 'We were both relatively young at thirty-eight, we were both businessmen with very similar philosophies in business, and we both wanted to strip the board down.' They worked on a plan to put before the club's shareholders that, in return for a loan of £100,000, they would get control for fifteen years. At first, it was to be a three-man board comprising the young tyros Lindsay, Robinson and Tom Rathbone, but Jack Hilton, the then chairman and a widely respected figure, joined the breakaway group and their success on an acrimonious night at Central Park was assured. Lindsay, who presented a highly articulate mission statement at that meeting, says: 'The supporters were looking for a change at the time, so they would probably have backed us in any case, but Jack's association with us was of enormous importance. More than that, his wisdom in the years that followed was invaluable to me. I have learnt more from Jack Hilton than anyone else about rugby league beyond the playing field.'

Lindsay's achievements at Wigan remain the most powerful testament to his abilities as an administrator. Although Hilton remained as chairman until Lindsay took over in 1986, it was patently clear that the younger man was the mover and shaker. Alex Murphy, a friend of Lindsay's who shared his passion for horse-racing, was appointed coach in the summer of 1982, and the following season led Wigan to triumph in the John Player Trophy. Remarkably, it was the first major trophy to be taken back to Central Park for fourteen years. Murphy lasted two seasons at Wigan, taking them to Wembley in 1984 where they were comprehensively beaten by Widnes, and departing after a heated exchange in the aftermath of a pre-season sevens tournament. Popular legend has it that Murphy threw a telephone at Lindsay, although both men later denied this happened. Already, Lindsay had displayed the ambition necessary to revive the town's interest in rugby league. He made a succession of major signings, and imported some of the best talent available. In 1984, he brought from Australia the winger John Ferguson and the stand-off Brett Kenny. They excited the Wigan public like no one since Billy Boston. 'I remember telling my father about John Ferguson,' Lindsay recalls. 'I told him that he must come and see him play. My father had gone to Wembley the previous season and had come away dreadfully disappointed when we were beaten by Widnes. I said that this year would be different. I could sense that we were going back to Wembley.' Lindsay arranged for his father to come to that weekend's game. Two days before the match, Nicholas Lindsay died. 'He never got to see us at Wembley that year when we beat Hull in one of the greatest finals ever. I regret that deeply.'

A succession of highly talented, highly prized players continued to make their way to Central Park: Ellery Hanley, Joe Lydon, Andy Gregory, Martin Offiah and Gary Connolly headed a long list of star recruits as the transfer record was broken with increasing regularity. Lindsay, while believing that the fundamental tenet of business is careful husbandry, was unafraid to lean on the instinct he developed at the racetrack, backed his judgement and, invariably, the gambles paid off. The wage bill spiralled, but so did attendances; not since the 1983–4 season has Wigan's average crowd over a season been less than 10,000. As he set out to do, Lindsay completely changed the culture of the club. The players were now well-paid, well-cared-for athletes, and respect between the team and the board was mutual. 'There was also a lot of fun,' adds Lindsay. 'That's why I liked being in charge at Wigan. I had lunatics around me like Joe Lydon and Andy Gregory. They were fantastic fun to be with. They also trusted me. I wouldn't say I was one of the lads but I was as close to them as it was possible to be.'

In 1986, Lindsay appointed a New Zealander, Graham Lowe, as coach, and a period of success unprecedented in the game was about to begin. In Lowe's first season at Central Park, Wigan took the League, the Premiership, the John Player Trophy and the Lancashire Cup. Strangely, they suffered defeat at Oldham in the first round of the Challenge Cup. Up until February 1996, when they were defeated at Salford, they won forty-three games in a row in the competition, taking the Cup an unprecedented eight times in succession. During that period, which saw four different coaches in charge, Wigan won enough trophies to fill a large removal van and gained worldwide reknown as the model professional organization. Paradoxically, this domination was recognized as one of the ills afflicting rugby league as it hurtled towards the Super

League. While only slightly taking the edge off the hunger for success of the Wigan public, the club's relentless supremacy gave every competition a predictability that diminished the game's overall appeal. In 1991, the engineer of one of the great sporting phenomena of our time was ready for higher office, and Lindsay was appointed president of the Rugby League and was chairman designate for the following year.

Towards the end of the 1991–2 season, Lindsay was in the French town of Albi for a Great Britain international. On the eve of the match, he went into town for a meal with Bob Ashby, then chairman of the league. They began to discuss who would replace David Oxley as chief executive when he retired later that year. Ashby suggested that Lindsay combine that job with the role of chairman. 'I didn't really want to do both jobs,' says Lindsay. 'I thought I would just be setting myself up to be shot down. But it did make me think. I'd had thirteen years at Wigan and I did fancy running the game. I could see the chief executive post becoming more important. Some weeks later, I told Bob that I wanted to pitch for it.' The position was advertised, 102 applications were received, and the board of directors spent three weeks interviewing candidates. At the end of the process, Lindsay was the unanimous choice and started work on 2 November 1992.

The difference between the two regimes was marked: Oxley, an urbane, laid-back man with an academic background had given way to a self-made businessman with a workaholic tendency. As one of the staff at rugby league headquarters said at the time: 'It was like going from a holiday camp to a concentration camp overnight.' Harry Gration says that Lindsay 'made it very clear that he was going to revolutionize the game. He was determined not to preside over its demise.' When he took over, Lindsay could hardly have foreseen the shape that the revolution would eventually assume.

There is a great deal of ambivalence about Lindsay in

rugby league circles. While some regard his unrelenting drive as representing a thirst for power, others see it as the quality that will take rugby league to the promised land. Those who have studied his management technique are agreed on one thing: he leaves no vacuum around or below him. 'He's a one-man band,' says Alex Murphy. 'I must admit he finds it difficult to delegate,' added Paul Harrison. 'The great thing about Maurice from my point of view,' says Vic Wakeling, the head of Sky Sports, 'is that he give me a decision any time of the day or night. He operates rather like a commissioner in American sport.'

Not even Rupert Murdoch, with the millions he has stumped up, has more at stake in the success of the Super League than Maurice Lindsay, the man who had a go.

SEVEN

NO TURNING BACK

The future is here. But will it work?

Maurice Lindsay walked across the car park at Central Park, Wigan, giving only terse answers to the journalists who were following him, climbed into his Jaguar and set off on the short trip to Aintree racecourse. It was around lunchtime on Saturday 8 April 1995 and Lindsay, chief executive of the rugby league, was heading for the Grand National. He permitted himself a smile of satisfaction; he had just received unanimous support from the club chairmen for a deal with Rupert Murdoch's News Corporation that would transform his sport and now he was on his way to watch one of his favourite events of the year. What's more, Lindsay could look forward to a lunch of poached salmon and Chablis at one of the hospitality suites overlooking the course. The man who had invited Lindsay, however, had rather less cause for happiness. Jonathan Martin, the head of BBC sport, was about to learn of the details of an agreement that could possibly torpedo the corporation's involvement with a sport that had consistently delivered good viewing figures. It might also set a trend in the relationship between sport and television that the BBC had little chance of following.

The deal, which gave News Corporation, the parent company of BSkyB, exclusive worldwide television rights to the proposed new Super League, did not in itself deal a major blow to the BBC. Although rugby league had been a regular feature of their Saturday afternoon *Grandstand* programme for more than three decades, they had lost the rights to broadcast league matches to Sky back in 1993. The BBC were left with the Challenge Cup and the Regal Trophy, for which they paid £500,000 a season. The putative contract with News Corporation, which at that point was worth £75 million, did not on the face of it weaken the BBC's portfolio. But, as well as raising the ante considerably, it presented a number of questions. If the sport moved to the summer, where would the Challenge Cup, the final of which provided one of *Grandstand*'s best days of the year, fit in the schedule? What would become of the Regal Trophy? Would the BBC even want a sport if it was being re-invented, and tenaciously marketed as such, by Sky? As the guests sat down to lunch in Martin's box at Aintree, the wider world was beginning to digest the news of what was a ground-breaking agreement.

It had a great many implications, even if it did not quite shake the foundations of sport like Sky's audacious coup of 1992 when they wrested the rights to live TV coverage of soccer from the terrestrial channels. Sky's £304 million deal had revolutionized English soccer. The Premier League was created and, with the massive injection of cash (the traditional channels had been used to paying a fraction of the amount Sky offered), clubs were able to tempt the best foreign players to Britain as well as putting money towards the renovation of stadiums that was a mandatory requirement of the Taylor Report. Suddenly, it seemed, the image of soccer changed and in polite circles the game became acceptable, even fashionable, again. Sky put considerable effort into making the sport look more exciting than it sometimes was, and while the hype was often tiresome, their technical expertise – many more cameras, new angles and action replays from different viewpoints – was applauded. Some of these innovations have since been copied by the BBC and ITV. David Hill, head of the BSkyB network when the deal was signed, said at the time that 'it was the biggest advance in TV football since the camera was invented'. Hill's successor, Sam Chisholm, also a plain-speaking Antipodean, said three years later that 'the benefits that have flowed to the clubs, the fans and the viewers are enormous'. Modesty never won a television audience but, allowing for the trademark hyperbole of statements to issue from company headquarters, it is undeniable that BSkyB certainly played a part in the rejuvenation of football in Britain in the Nineties.

More significant, perhaps, was the transformation of BSkyB's fortunes wrought by the Premiership deal. In 1992, the network was losing money, sales of satellite dishes were not growing at the anticipated rate, and consequently advertising revenues were low. They needed a major property, one that would be immediately translated into sales of dishes. Football provided the answer, but for the first time armchair followers of the game had to fork out for their entertainment: first, they had to buy a dish and then pay a subscription fee. By 1996, BSkyB had 3.2 million subscribers, a growth rate of around 20 per cent a year, and, following a successful flotation on the stock market in 1994, became Britain's most profitable broadcaster. Their operating profits rose to around £1 billion a year. Roger Devlin of Henry Ansbacher, a company that gives financial advice to a number of top football clubs, said: 'There is a growing awareness in the football industry about just how critical football has been to Sky's success.' Sport, even more than the purchasing of blockbuster films for the movie channels, moved dishes, and, in the wake of Premiership football, Ryder Cup golf, England's overseas cricket tours (which had never been covered on terrestrial TV), some of the big fights, and live Courage League rugby union moved on to satellite. Rugby league, meanwhile, was the first sport to sign a deal with the fledgling British Satellite Broadcasting channel when it launched in April 1990. This contract, which covered league matches, was taken over when Sky and BSB merged seven months later, and prior to the Super League arrangement, was worth £4 million over three years. The deal signed with the BBC in 1992 was for live coverage of the Challenge Cup and Regal Trophy matches.

Rugby league has traditionally had an ambivalent attitude towards television. The first match to be broadcast nationally by the BBC was a Test between Great Britain and New Zealand in 1951. By the end of the Fifties, the sport had become a regular part of the corporation's sports output. Clearly, national coverage did much to raise the game's profile, but it also had a seriously negative effect on attendance figures. The loss of revenue through the turnstiles was not counterbalanced by the money paid for the rights. The argument over the pros and cons of television raged throughout the game, and in 1960, the rugby league decided to halt the live coverage of matches. Crowds that season were the worst of the postwar period. Bill Fallowfield, then secretary of the league and one of the game's TV pioneers, wrote in the aftermath of the campaign that 'it would be foolish to argue that television, or the lack of it, was wholly responsible for this state of affairs. It does, however, support the view that the televising of matches is doing no further harm to the game. The showing of the game to millions of viewers has, of course, created a more widespread interest, and there has certainly been an impact in the south.' Cameras were back the next season.

Throughout the Sixties, the relationship between the sport and the BBC was testy; Wigan prohibited cameras from their ground for a Challenge Cup tie in 1966, while in 1969, a cabal of sixteen clubs went to the courts in an ultimately unsuccessful effort to ban coverage of their games. Rugby league's unrest was rooted in two major concerns. The main worry was the financial equation; there was a feeling that the BBC were getting the game on the cheap, that the money they were putting in was no recompense for the hit clubs were taking in gate receipts. Second, there was the manner of presentation. Way back in the Fifties, Fallowfield told a meeting of the rugby league council that 'the public were not happy with the commentaries'. Eddie Waring was the BBC's self-proclaimed 'Mr Rugby League', a man who had impeccable credentials in the game as a successful coach and manager of Dewsbury and later as a much-travelled journalist. But the mudlark image he often presented of the game was felt to do it a grave disservice. The notes on the author for the 1966 volume *The Eddie Waring Book of Rugby League* give a clear indication of the tone he adopted in his broadcasts, and the light in which he was viewed. 'A columnist with the *Sunday Mirror*, his racy television commentaries are listened to by thousands who do so for no other reason than the human touch he brings to an often seemingly inhuman game.' In short, while he may have been the toast of living rooms in Weybridge, he set teeth on edge in Wakefield. Maurice Lindsay believes that Waring's commentaries 'may have set the game back twenty years'. This is possibly a revisionist theory, however, and there is an argument that this likeable, extremely knowledgeable light entertainer who was regularly popping up on game shows or with Morecambe and Wise did more to spread the rugby league gospel than any of the half-baked schemes to establish the game outside its traditional boundaries.

Nevertheless, there is a significant body of opinion in the north that the BBC, viewed as the epitome of the antipathetic public school establishment, were happy to portray rugby league for many years as an oafish game not to be taken too seriously. This, of course, was in contrast to the altogether slicker, more reverent presentation of the amateur game. ('We were for a long time the poor relations as far as the BBC were concerned,' said Lindsay. When Eddie Waring retired in 1981 at the age of seventy-five, he was replaced by Ray French, a St Helens schoolteacher and a man who played both codes of rugby. Matters improved, but only up to a point. 'Would the BBC have picked Ray French if he hadn't had such a strong northern accent?' is Lindsay's rhetorical question. Furthermore, the effort put into presentation still lagged some way behind rugby union, and there was little commitment to the sport beyond covering games. Rugby union had its own magazine programme on Sunday afternoons; for years, the BBC did not even broadcast the results of rugby league matches. Nevertheless, the BBC have raised their game considerably in recent times, even if some of the improvements they introduced – like the use of touchline reporters and multi-angle replays – were directly borrowed from Sky. The introduction as a pundit of John Monie, then the Wigan coach and an articulate, highly knowledgeable figure, did much to improve the quality of coverage.

It would be simplistic to believe that rugby league was driven into Sky's arms by the injustice, real or perceived, in their treatment by the BBC, but when Maurice Lindsay was on his way to Aintree, a conversation with Jonathan Martin three years previously was playing back in his head. The two parties were in Leeds negotiating for the renewal of the BBC contract. Lindsay, newly appointed as chief executive and determined to eke more money out of the deal, pressed Martin to raise the fee. 'There's no competition for the rights,' said Martin. 'Come back to me when there's some competition.' In the intervening three years, the whole relationship between sport and television had changed.

'Rugby league does all right for us. It doesn't do great business, but it does good business,' says Vic Wakeling, the head of Sky Sports. 'Football is way out in front for us, then there are the big fights, but after that, rugby league, cricket and golf are all on a par. It depends on the event.' Accurate viewing figures for Sky broadcasts are notoriously difficult to gather, but it is believed that live Friday night matches are watched by an audience of 100,000. The best matches, it is believed, can pull in 200,000. Clearly, Sky have hopes that, for their £87 million investment, figures for the Super League will be higher. Rugby league has been a very good performer for the BBC in recent years, and audiences compare favourably with those for the top rugby union matches. In 1995, for instance, the union international between Wales and South Africa drew 3.42 million viewers, England v. Canada was watched by 3.8 million, Wales v. England by 4.65 million and England v. Scotland by 7.27 million. A rugby league match between Castleford and Halifax got an audience of 3.87 million, the Challenge Cup tie between Wigan and St Helens drew 4.28 million, while the World Cup Final pulled in 4.86 million. 'It is perceived as a two-county sport,' explains Wakeling, 'but when run-of-the mill Regal Trophy matches are not far behind Five Nations' internationals in terms of viewing figures, it clearly has an appeal beyond the rugby league enthusiast. The fact is that it is a good TV sport. It's an easy game to understand and, even if you don't understand the intricacies, you can sit back and enjoy the pace and the power.'

The disparity between Sky's rugby league audience and the BBC's explains why there is anxiety within the game that the ties with terrestrial television should not be severed. Built into the Premiership football deal was the subletting of rights to the BBC which, in effect, restored *Match of the Day* to Saturday nights. It was sensed at the time that if football disappeared from the majority of the nation's screens, the resultant loss of visibility would have an adverse effect on attendances and media profile. Rugby league can afford even less to diminish its impact on the national consciousness. Nevertheless, Sky's immediate objective is to make the Super League work. 'We're in it for five years and we believe we can help the clubs,' explains Wakeling. 'For one, we're giving them a lot of money. Two, we're actually going to promote the game because we need rugby league to do well for us. We have a good marketing and promotion department here who are working with the league on everything from selling the individual games to designing the trophies. We are in a partnership but it's a hell of a punt.'

Wakeling believes that much rests on the success of the Super League in London and Paris. 'If they don't work, where are we? We're left with a regional sport that isn't going anywhere. We need it to catch on there if we are going to have another successful sport. Paris is important because, in a cosmetic way, it brings some glamour to the league. London is crucial in spreading the game, and it worries me a little bit. We need them to do well. If it doesn't work out for them at Charlton, then you've got to say in a couple of years that they should have another go in another part of London.' As for Paris, he said that their first task was to ensure TV coverage. 'I told Paris that they should aim to get a partner, someone who will broadcast games and put some promotional effort behind the sport. I said that they shouldn't worry about selling the rights – it's not worth anything to anyone. For the first year at least, there will probably be no money from that deal coming back into News Corporation.'

Partnership is something of a corporate buzzword for Sky, and Wakeling reacts strongly to suggestions that they will play the lead role in determining the future direction of rugby league. 'We will be involved in a constant dialogue. We intend to work hand in hand with the sport,' he explains. 'There are two different relationships between sport and TV: there's the traditional relationship with the terrestrial channels and there's a Sky relationship. The terrestrial channels are not interested in support programmes – they only want to cherry-pick certain events. We can offer a lot more than money. A lot of sports come to ask if we can do the same for them that we have done with the Premiership. Everyone quotes the

Premiership deal as an example of how to get it right. Our initial contract with football was for nine hours a week, but we actually do eighteen hours because it works for us. We are the only channel who has ever given rugby league its own magazine programme. We find that we get on better with sports bodies because they see that we put in some effort beyond just covering matches. We work with them in selling the games.' Wakeling adds that part of this dialogue includes taking the advice of experts. 'Originally,' he says, 'we wanted Super League games on Monday nights to run on from our Monday night football programme. This was felt by people in the game to be a bad idea because they didn't think the crowds would be there. So we abandoned the plan.' The live Super League games are now on Friday and Saturday evenings.

Sky, naturally, are concerned that the backdrop for the Super League meets the expectations fuelled by Sky's strident promotional activities. 'I am worried about some of the grounds, and particularly about the standard of the floodlights,' concedes Wakeling. 'Without vivid pictures, the game can look drab.' He is also concerned about the crowds. 'If you haven't got bums on seats in the stadiums, we haven't good a good atmosphere, and sport without atmosphere is a loser for everyone.' He stresses the need for marketing on a local as well as national level, and explained that in the first season of the Premiership, a huge effort was made to attract crowds to the Monday night games with the Sky Strikers – a dancing troupe – and firework displays. This was not to everyone's taste – on one of the pre-game shows, the Southampton secretary said that "one old lady phoned to say that the fireworks made her cat bolt out of the door and she hasn't seen it since" – but attendances on Monday nights showed an increase on the corresponding fixtures the previous season.'

Sky have a budget of £3.5 million to promote the Super League, and the Rugby League have retained 7.5 per cent of the money due to the clubs as part of the News Corporation contract to help pay for local marketing. The cheer-leading, however, will not erase some genuine worries about rugby league's new 'partnership'. Editorial objectivity was the first casualty in Sky's presentation of the Super League deal. When the controversy over the proposed mergers was at its peak, the station filmed a vox pop of fans to get their views. Each one was overwhelmingly positive; they could see nothing but good in the plans. The interviews were filmed in Wigan, well removed from the epicentre of protest. 'It was a big mistake,' admits Wakeling. 'You would expect the fans in Wigan to be fully behind the Super League. We looked stupid.' He says that, thereafter, 'we got involved in balanced debate. We did allow a couple of chairmen who were against it, and a few fans, to have their say.' Nevertheless, on the final day of the first Super League season, the Sky cameras were out again to collect the views of the 'fans'. Again, they came back with wholly supportive opinions. And again, almost all the fans they asked were supporters of Wigan and St Helens on their way to watch their teams contest the Premiership. At the end of the Premiership, the Sky cameras panned across the crowd and focused on a family, cheerfully waving to the players. 'This is the smiling face of the Super League,' asserted Eddie Hemmings, the Sky commentator. 'And that's all because we've moved to the summer,' he added. But wasn't this a man's game for all the family two decades earlier? Hasn't the atmosphere on the terraces always been unthreatening and family-friendly? Murdoch's money may have changed the game; it's not yet changed the people who watch it.

Discussion between Hemmings and his co-presenter Mike Stephenson was invariably superficial and often embarrassingly one-sided. 'Let's get positive,' was Stephenson's stock reply to any criticism. As Giles Smith in the *Independent on Sunday* said, discussions took the form of 'assertion masquerading as conversation'. While Wakeling, a man who learnt his trade on national newspapers, believes the coverage must have integrity, he says honestly: 'We are not going to criticize Super League, because we believe in it.' Equally worrying was an incident towards the end of the centenary season. At the conclusion of Sky's Sunday night programme came the results of that day's matches. The scores of the Super League teams, and from the First Division, were given, but those from the third round of the Challenge Cup, involving the Second Division clubs, were not. The message was: it's not a competition shown on Sky, and therefore it doesn't exist. It is a form of news management that, given Murdoch also controls four of Britain's biggest national newspapers, understandably causes creeping anxieties. To emphasize the point, Sky's Super League coverage is sponsored by *The Times*, a newspaper owned by Murdoch.

But these concerns are an insignificant part of the global picture. The deal between News Corporation and rugby league broke the mould, illustrating that sport is no different from any other commodity. It could be bought and sold on the open market. Many feel that this can only benefit sport: because of the lack of competition, television has purchased the rights on the cheap for too long. Why shouldn't any sport maximize its earning potential? And why shouldn't those who want to watch it in the comfort of their living rooms pay for the privilege? These questions have been taken to both Houses of Parliament, and the issue of saving the major sports events for the nation (or at least the vast majority who have not yet been driven to buying a satellite dish, or who can't afford one) has gained a political importance.

The protected status of certain events as defined by the 1990 Broadcasting Act – England's home cricket Test matches, the Derby and the Grand National, football's World Cup Finals, the FA Cup Final and the Scottish FA Cup Final, and the Finals weekend at Wimbledon – can last for only so long. In many ways we are defined as a nation by our sporting heritage, and it's only right that it should be preserved for the nation. We cannot leave our sports to the mercy of a media mogul. No turning back, insists the Sky network's self-promotion. There will certainly be no turning back for rugby league. Either the Super League works, or the game may dead, or even eaten alive by rugby union. Rugby league, through its financial weakness, probably didn't have a choice but to take Murdoch's money. Others do.

Just after the Super League became a reality, Eddie Hemmings and Mike 'Stevo' Stephenson, the Saint and Greavsie of Sky's rugby league coverage, attempted an objective discussion about the merits of the new structure.

Eddie: 'It's got to be right, hasn't it?'

Stevo: 'It's all about making a great spectacle, so thumbs up.'

Allowing for Sky's stake in making the future work, this level of partiality did neither the game nor the satellite channel any favours. The outrage that many felt about the way their game had been turned on its head overnight was exacerbated by the sense that there was no chance for serious debate of the issues, and that too many vested interests were given a mouthpiece. As a result, much of the discussion within the game was heated and represented the extremes of opinion. Ten months after the deal was signed, I canvassed these views from a broad spectrum of interested parties. I believe they present an accurate picture of the concerns and anxieties, hopes and ambitions felt at all levels of the game . . .

Geoffrey Moorhouse, author and lifelong Wigan supporter: 'I look to the future with great trepidation. I am deeply worried about

Rupert Murdoch's level of control. I wouldn't trust Murdoch further than I could spit or perform any other bodily function. The way I can see the game going is as an Australian version of gridiron football. Changing the club names is the least of it; squad numbering and the unlimited interchangeability of players are to be introduced, and there was a report that the Australians are to consider allowing a forward pass on the fifth tackle. That would be American football without the shoulder pads. We have already travelled some way along this road, and the game now, magnificently athletic though it is, bears little resemblance to the one I fell in love with many years ago. I am agnostic about the move to the summer, because as I get older I less enjoy sitting in the cold. And some of our traditions are being devalued in any case. I went to the last Boxing Day fixture between Wigan and St Helens and was utterly disgusted that Saints played their second team because their eyes were on a bigger prize. I walked out at half-time. I felt that if the top clubs could be so contemptuous of our traditions, why should we bother fighting to preserve them? It is often difficult to separate the soppy sentimentality from the good things about the game, but the major quality of rugby league was that the club genuinely represented the community, and the players behaved themselves. They didn't bare their arses to the crowd or intimidate referees. It was sad that it didn't spread beyond the heartland but that idea was meretricious and vastly overrated anyway. What I fear is that Rupert Murdoch will drop the game immediately if it is not performing in his terms. And then what are we left with? The traditions will have been dismantled and true supporters will have been alienated to such an extent that they have turned to cricket. I see the only way forward to be a merger with rugby union, but probably on their terms. If we end up with a winter game called rugby that's 13-a-side, with line-outs, I'll be happy. Rugby league's epitaph? It was the last game to be corrupted by money.'

David Oxley, former secretary of the rugby league: 'The future is unknown, but what was certain was that the game couldn't go on as it was. Two-thirds of clubs were in serious financial trouble, and the crisis had reached such proportions that we were in danger of losing some of them for ever. When Murdoch came along out of the blue, professional rugby league was in bigger trouble than at any time in its history. Perhaps we could have extracted more money from the deal, particularly when you see what is being offered for the Five Nations' Championship, but the clubs were put under enormous time pressure. But now that we have it, the money must be used sensibly, on the development of the game at junior levels and on the improvement of stadiums. I think mistakes have been made along the way to Super League. The thought that mergers could be forced through was ill-judged and, predictably, caused a very powerful reaction. Also, we had the scandal of the centenary season that never was. The centenary, which had been planned for five years or more, could have been used to bring prestige and income into the game. Instead, we had this hybrid season that was simply a bad rehearsal for the Super League, and which saw many fans voting with their feet and staying away. I have never witnessed so much apathy from rugby league supporters and the game will have a big job to persuade them back for the Super League. My biggest worry, however, is what's happening to the game itself. We seem to have gone too far in the restless search to make play more continuous. It has become faster and faster, and we have lost the peaks and troughs that were essential to the appeal of the game. Unlimited substitutions, the introduction of four quarters (which will surely come) mean that players and spectators rarely have a chance to catch their breath. I'm not sure we want 64–42 scorelines. So are we making a false assumption that we have the product to win a new public? I also think moving to summer is based on a dangerous illusion that there are thousands of potential spectators who will be tempted in July in a way they weren't in November. Facilities have to be improved: a lousy stadium in the winter is a lousy stadium in the summer, too.'

Peter Fox, former coach of Bradford Northern: 'We desperately needed the money, but I think it was grabbed without thinking. The question of clubs merging was handled badly. I think the game will narrow down eventually; for instance, one day a local entrepreneur will arrive on the scene and propose the merger of Castleford, Wakefield and Featherstone, playing on a brand new ground, and together they could form a very strong combination. We should be concentrating on these areas where the grass roots are strong, instead of trying to spread out over the country. Also, I don't think we know what we have taken on with moving to the summer. I used to dread Easter time, playing on hard grounds with very little grass. Also, if we get summers as hot as 1995, what about the players getting dehydrated? The game is so fast these days. Ever since 1980, the accent has been on fitness. If I was to pick a team from scratch today, I'd choose eleven players who were over 6 feet, more than 13 stone, who were fast and strong, and two – a half-back and a hooker – who were thinkers and manipulators who could handle the ball. The game today has become too predictable. There is a definite feeling that it is more designed for television than the spectators. I am something of a traditionalist, and while I can see the commercial reasons for altering the club names, this half-hearted Americanism is not for me. I remember that when I was appointed coach at Bradford, I stood alone on the terraces at Odsal and thought that this was the ground where I had seen my brothers play international matches, where I had seen my first floodlit game, and now I was the coach of

Bradford Northern. It was a dream name – Bradford Northern. I was proud to be associated with such an historic name. I am quite happy not be associated with Bradford Bulls.'

Peter Higham, chairman of Warrington: 'The game is at the crossroads, particularly in respect to its relationship with rugby union. I am very worried about clubs forging links with rugby union, like Wigan allowing Orrell to play at their ground, or Leeds inviting the Leeds rugby union club to use Headingley and even offering the prospect of lending them players, or matches between league and union clubs. If we go too far down that road, there is a distinct chance that we will be subject to a take-over and our game will disappear for ever. There is still a layer of management in rugby union that detests rugby league and everything that it stands for, and our top clubs have got to decide whether they want to be playing in the Super League or the Courage League Division One. We have a good game that belongs to the players and the supporters. It doesn't belong to people who seem happy to sell out for thirty pieces of silver. We had a chance, with the money coming in from Murdoch, to concentrate our resources on the top clubs, but already that sum has been watered down. We still seem to be subsidizing the lower clubs. We must compete at the highest level, and our main competition is with rugby union. We have to give summer rugby a go, because people weren't coming in the winter. I know there's a breed of spectator who likes standing in the pouring rain but in Warrington, there's 200,000 who don't, and who might be persuaded to come in the summer if they are comfortable, and they can have a drink and a meal. One of the reasons attendances have fallen is that there is less variety in the game these days; if a team gets 55 per cent possession and doesn't make too many mistakes, they will win the game, whereas in the recent past you could win a game with 30 per cent of the ball. You just defended and defended, and it made for more absorbing contests. But now we must look five years ahead and certain disciplines in terms of development have to be implemented. Otherwise, rugby union will take us over. We have to be strong, or we'll get murdered.'

David Storey, author of *This Sporting Life*: 'I mourn the transformation of rugby league from a community-based sport to another branch of the entertainment industry, which has its own dynamic. But money directs the attention in an alien direction, and it has an unstoppable force. I used to think of rugby league as an extension of the coalmining industry, not just in terms of its geography, but it has the same mechanical, repetitive process. Tackle, play-the-ball, tackle – it has a similar rhythm to chipping away at rocks. But now, of course, the coalmining has gone, and so has the confederacy that infused the game in the Fifties and Sixties, the camaraderie that came from a united struggle, whether it be against nature or the class system. It looks romantic now, but it was very tangible then. Players are more mobile now, on short-term contracts, and the game itself has been integrated into the suburbanization of regional activities. I have always been attracted by the dispassionate element of sport, the fact that you are competing purely against the opposition. When that competitiveness becomes related more to money, and then to showbiz and display, it loses much of its validity.'

Jonathan Davies, former union and league international: 'The clubs had no choice but to take the money, and now they have five years to sort themselves out and see what happens. The proof of the pudding as far as Super League is concerned will be at the end of the five-year contract. I can't see there being any merger between the codes in that period. There is just too much tradition and too many vested interests on both sides for that to happen quickly. Who will rule on whether we have line-outs or six tackles? I suppose money will in the end decide which way we go. But even that is difficult to forecast, because in the northern hemisphere rugby union has the power and the money, whereas in the southern hemisphere, it is league. Rugby league has certainly adapted better recently in making itself more attractive – moving scrums infield and increasing the yardage gap at the play-the ball – and moving to the summer will be better for the spectators. But it will be harder for the players, particularly in the first season when the grounds will not have had the chance to recover.'

Ray French, BBC commentator and former St Helens player: 'We are taking a step into the great unknown, but the game needed a dramatic shake-up in its approach. The Murdoch money has enabled this to happen and if the game can't take full advantage of the £87 million, then it doesn't deserve to succeed. At least, it will mean that some clubs can emerge from the ice age as far as their attitude towards the media and public relations is concerned. In the past, PR consisted of having someone answering a phone and then not knowing the answer, or putting up a poster in a sweet shop advertising the next match. More effort will be spent on selling the game. I still favour a winter season, but I think the experiment is worthwhile as it may attract new people into the game. However, I am not in favour of the proliferation of night matches. Habits have changed over the past few decades, and the trend these days on summer evenings is for barbecues or sitting in the garden with a drink. I don't know whether people will fancy going over to Hull for a 6 o'clock kick-off. I also think it is a myth that great games can only be played in good weather. Great games can take place in snow, rain and wind and we may lose a lot of individual skills if the accent is purely on fast, superfit robots. That was never the intention of the sport. Nevertheless, being in the summer allows us to escape from under the umbrella of rugby union. We have always been in the shadow of union in terms of media coverage, and we will not now have to compete with them.

However, if rugby league disappears from terrestrial TV, I think we will have a big problem. Clearly I speak as a BBC man, but as our game does not have a national identity, we cannot afford to be closeted away on satellite television. Our impact could suffer dramatically; Sky's viewing figures are around 100,000 whereas we get 5 million watching on a Saturday afternoon. That means a lot for the consciousness of the game. We need to reach a wider audience, but we have rarely looked beyond our horizons. We have never commanded the capital city. Odd though it may seem, I relate it to literature in the fourteenth century. Chaucer lived in London, near the printing presses, near the money, and his poetry became famous; a Lancashire poet wrote *Sir Gawayne and the Green Knight*, easily the equal of anything Chaucer wrote, and he remains unknown to this day. If you don't command the capital city, you don't have a chance. Now, rugby union has the power base, but after a hundred years of fighting against them, we are putting the welcome mat out for them, allowing them to use our grounds, and allowing our players to join them. Economically, the two games will eventually be forced together but for the five-year period of the Super League, I believe the status quo will be preserved. The sixth year, however, could see some quite dramatic change.'

Colin Welland, playwright and former president of Fulham: 'I find the whole situation in both codes of rugby exciting, after a hundred years of being set in concrete. These are fantastic times, and we must begin by repairing the breach with rugby union. They have too much wealth and too great a power base for us to fight them. That's not to suggest that we should go cap in hand to rugby union. After all, we've something they want – our players are better, our rules are better, and our game is more entertaining to watch. We have the product, but they have the clout. In any case, it was a totally artificial schism in the first place, and although the games developed on different cultural lines, the split has been based on prejudice and bigotry. There is nothing now to sustain the division. Rugby union clubs could enter teams in the summer Super League and eventually it will become nonsense at the highest level to have two distinctively separate sports. There should be one game of rugby and it would be good enough and strong enough to challenge soccer's supremacy. It should be like a marriage between the two games – there has to be give and take. It hurts me to see 75,000 at Twickenham watching that crap, but at least now they know it's crap. At an England international in 1996, the people around me were shouting: 'Bring on Wigan.' Their game is ripe for the plucking. It is sad when we are thinking of giving up our traditions, but rugby league has not really progressed. In fact, it has gone backward in terms of security. That's why there was no alternative to taking the Murdoch money. I wish it hadn't been him, but sentiment cannot rule reality and the plan was passed unanimously by the people in the game who knew exactly what the financial situation was. The mergers were presented in a clumsy way, but there's no doubt that Wakefield and Featherstone, for instance, would be a viable proposition if they joined forces. On their own, it's hard to see how they have a future. What worries me is the introduction of more influences from Australia. Unlimited substitutions raises the spectre of offensive and defensive units, and all that nonsense from American football. But new rugby league is a bit like New Labour; I may not approve of all the changes, but they'll still have my allegiance. And never has a bold step been taken without risk.'

Eric Ashton, chairman of St Helens: 'We were never going to get anywhere if we continued to look back. We had to look forward. I have a few worries about playing in the summer, but the spectators are certainly going to see better rugby. And if we can get 5,000 people to watch on a freezing cold day, we must stand a chance of attracting bigger crowds when it's shirtsleeve order. But the idea is to get new people on the terraces, and we've all appointed chief executives and marketing managers, so it's now up to them to sell the game. My biggest fear is that we don't have enough good players. Most of them are concentrated at one club, and the rest are spread around. I would like to have seen fewer teams in the Super League. But the mergers weren't presented in the right way. We were all rushed into signing the deal, having been told that if we don't sign today, it will be taken away tomorrow. The game was at such a low ebb, that we couldn't afford to say no. But it was definitely wrong to decide all these things overnight.'

Robin Whitfield, former player and referee: 'I think there is a grander game plan than has been generally recognized. The Super League is merely a stepping stone to a world league, which will involve the best handful of clubs in Britain playing against the Australian and New Zealand clubs. The rest of British rugby league will be in a sorry mess. Already there are worries being expressed by a number of the clubs in the First Division that, even if they finish in the top position, they might not get promoted to the Super League if it means the likes of London and Paris losing their spot or if a new team from, say, Newcastle or Birmingham wanted to join. They don't have relegation in the Australian competition – and that really is a competition – and it may be the way we'll go over here. I believe that the first season of Super League could be an embarrassment, with huge scores and massive victories. That will have people switching off their televisions in droves. However, games between Wigan and Manly, or Leeds and Canberra, or St Helens and Auckland will fill stadiums and have people clamouring for satellite dishes. And that, after all, is what it's all about. The end of season play-offs between British and Australian clubs which are sure to produce terrific games will, I believe, be the first step towards a world league. They won't necessarily play every week, but it will be a big event when they do. Over there, they have sixteen teams who can give Wigan a game – we've got maybe two or three. Summer rugby will be better for the spectators, but the biggest competition will come from tradition. Rugby league in the winter represents a hundred years of habit; it is part of our lives. But are the people running the game really concerned about attendances? What they want is to promote the selling of dishes. Murdoch needs to get a return on his investment. I am all for progress, but we are not walking towards it, but running, what with more officials on the pitch and cameras deciding on whether a try was scored or not. Where will it all end? We are going like American football and it worries me because that's not the game I know.'

Kath Hetherington, president of the Rugby League: 'I have long been an advocate of summer rugby. Moving to the summer, in addition to improving our facilities, will make it easier to attract new spectators to the game. It is essential that we broaden our appeal – many of our traditional supporters are middle-aged to old, and we must bring in more families and younger people. There was no question that we had to accept the money. When you win the lottery, you are not usually tempted to send the money back. I also think mergers were the way forward. We may not have envisaged the wave of feeling in small communities, but in the end that's all it was – a wave of feeling. Mergers cannot be made to happen, but I am sure some will evolve within the initial five-year run of the Super League. Take Halifax and Huddersfield, for instance. The two towns virtually run into each other, and yet Halifax has a Super League team and an old ground while Huddersfield has a magnificent stadium and no Super League team. A city of the size of Hull could surely support a Super League club, but they don't have one. It is only entrenched loyalties and traditions that are barring the way. But not all traditions are necessarily good. Rugby league may be a community-based game, but there will always be community teams. There may eventually be only one professional club in the Castleford, Wakefield and Featherstone area, but the game will still be played at a lower level within those towns. We need to look to a new market, to spread the game nationally, and this deal gives us the chance to do just that.'

Daryl Powell, Keighley Cougars and Great Britain stand-off: 'The vast majority of players have welcomed the move to summer. The fixture schedule will be less demanding, as it will take away all the midweek games caused through postponements, and the grounds will be in better condition. It will be a lot better than trudging through the mud, and training will certainly be a lot more pleasurable. Fewer fixtures may mean that some clubs will find it difficult to get enough gate money, but the quality should improve and, after all, the Australians have survived on relatively few games. But the sport has gone through a difficult period, and of paramount importance now is the need for stability. We must get through the first couple of seasons without any major dramas. I think a lot of supporters, particularly the older ones, have been turned off by the arguing and the politics over the Super League. There is also a lot of cynicism over the fact that we have been seen to sell out to one man, or at least one organization. Other sports believe that we have sold out to TV, and we must be careful not to lose our identity. We must also try to keep the Cup competitions on terrestrial TV – that's the only way we will have a hook into the south.'

Graeme West, coach of Wigan: 'If we are to match the Australians, we had to go forward. And if that means a break with tradition, then I think it is acceptable. Tradition can make things stagnant, and the move to summer will certainly help players develop their skills, as well as suiting the spectators, particularly the older ones. I also think it makes commercial sense to number the first twenty-five players on your squad. Kids like buying the shirt of their favourite player; in America, everyone knows what number Michael Jordan has. However, I am against the idea of unlimited substitutes, because it can add unnecessary complications. I voted for having four substitutes and six changes. The coming together of league and union holds out some exciting prospects and over the next few years there are sure to be some interesting experiments, perhaps using hybrid rules. Who knows what will happen? The two codes were together in the first place, so perhaps they will be again. I hope the Super League provides stronger competition, but if it doesn't there will be a need for fine tuning, which may result in clubs merging. In Hawera, my own home town in New Zealand which has a population of only 8,000, there were two rugby union clubs that were going nowhere, so in the past year, they merged, took in some of the satellite clubs in the area and now they have a much stronger club. This may be the way forward in Britain. If clubs are determined not to merge, they have to find other ways of making themselves more competitive by increasing their commercial efforts and getting more youngsters in the area playing the game. I would like to see more money ploughed into junior development. In five years' time, we must have more players to choose from.'

Harry Edgar, editor of *Open Rugby*, rugby league's monthly magazine: 'There is a huge amount of negativism among supporters, and this has been bred both by uncertainty and a lack of confidence in the game's administration to get things right. Even some of those running top clubs are unsure about what's happening. This could all have been avoided if the right choices had been made five years ago. In the late

Eighties, rugby league was on something of a high: we had learned lessons from the Australians, crowds were on the increase, our media profile was much better, amateur leagues were starting up all over the country and rugby union was in a trough. There was a real feeling of optimism within the game. But the potential was not translated into reality. If we had adopted a sensible fixture structure, reducing the number of meaningless games, and backed it up by selling the game in a more professional way, we might not have been in the position where there was no option but to take the money. I am not against the switch to summer in principle, but I don't see how putting on a bit of razzmatazz and pre-match entertainment will get the crowds flocking back. And I don't agree that playing in the winter means smaller crowds. Boxing Day attendances are often the best of the season. And in American football, teams like Buffalo and Green Bay, who play in uncovered stadiums often in temperatures well below freezing, sell out every one their games. That's because the game is an important thing for the local community. We needed to sell rugby league, to give it a similar importance. And we never did – we have just paid lip service to public relations. Take the way the mergers were presented. You can't just tell teams to merge or die. I don't see why we couldn't have had a Super League playing in the summer and the rest of the league – acting as feeder clubs, perhaps – playing in the winter. As it stands now, we have handed rugby union a tremendous opportunity because they have access to our public. And if they start playing on rugby league grounds, there is a real possibility that many of our traditional supporters could be converted. There is a great deal of fear for the future.'

So what are we to make of all this? As Stevo would say to Eddie: 'It's a game of opinions.' But there is common thread to all the views, whether they be optimistic or doom-laden. Harry Edgar, a man closely in touch with the feelings of rugby league's genuine supporters, used a powerful four-letter word: fear. I would second that emotion, and most of those I have talked to in the course of completing this book would admit to varying degrees of trepidation about the future. For some, it is a pessimism based on the painful experiences of the past. Rugby league has tried many times to reinvent itself, has attempted to conquer virgin territory on several occasions and has meddled with the rules and the structure endlessly but, after a hundred years of repeated and often turbulent change, we still found ourselves anchored to our roots with a game that couldn't afford to pay the electric bill. Others feel the shadow of rugby union looming as it never has before. The dismantling of the barricades that existed between the two codes has opened up dizzying possibilities, one of which is that union, a truly national game with access to serious riches and a steady supply of millionaires ready to bankroll it, can use its greater strength to coerce rugby league out of existence at the top level. This process may have already begun with the sharing of grounds and the invitation for league players to hop over the fence in the winter.

It is not only a partisan opinion that the rules of league provide for a more attractive game, for spectators and television alike, but if union were to make adjustments (like reducing the number of players, and possibly removing the line-out) a further reason for the codes to co-exist would be removed. Jonathan Davies suggests that money will decide, and that is increasingly the case in modern sport. What's to stop a mogul with TV interests buying up the best teams in both games and starting up a unified game? After all, it is only a step removed from what Rupert Murdoch has done with rugby league in Britain and Australia. If league lost its best clubs to another competition, or even found its best players tempted by bigger pay packets elsewhere, the future for the rump of the game would be bleak indeed. There would be enough loyalists to ensure that the flame was kept alive in the bedrock areas of West Yorkshire or south Lancashire, but probably only on a level akin to the lower divisions of rugby union's present-day Courage League.

Colin Welland puts forward a convincing case that one game is what we should all be striving towards, but he would like the dominance of soccer to be challenged. This may represent modern thinking, but the overwhelming feeling of a majority of supporters is that, whatever greater cause may be served, they don't want a meaningful part of their lives to be bartered away. They have seen Murdoch arrive, call the tune, and some believe that the club chairmen played the rats to his Pied Piper. It sticks in the craw that a game which, over a century, has survived through a manful struggle against injustice and prejudice could be bought and sold overnight. It simply doesn't wash that the deal merely represents the selling of television rights. And there is little validity in the view that rugby league now controls its own destiny. Murdoch can pull the plug in five years' time, probably earlier if he so wishes, so to a great extent the game depends on the patronage of a man for whom economics is the god. That cannot be a healthy state of affairs for any sport.

We do, however, have an opportunity. The Murdoch money must not be allowed simply to slip into the pockets of players, or be used to pay the salaries of a new breed of chief executives and marketing managers, or be frittered away on half-baked promotional initiatives, or be allowed to prop up London and Paris if they appear to be failing. It must be put towards the refurbishment of stadiums, development of the game at junior levels, and to nourish clubs where there is proven potential, even if they are outside the Super League. To borrow the portentous phrase used by Sky to introduce its rugby league coverage, we must seize the day. Otherwise, someone else will seize the game.

During the hundred-year lifespan of rugby league, the people of the north of England have survived great economic pressures and withstood many social injustices. For many, the disappearance of a game that has come to symbolize much of what the region stands for would be a cut too deep. We can see it happening and this is why we are scared. The cotton mills have long since closed down. The pit winding gear is now silent. The quality of life has suffered repeated erosions. We are right to fear the loss of the greatest game.

All Pan Books are available at your local bookshop or newsagent, or can be ordered direct from the publisher. Indicate the number of copies required and fill in the form below.

Send to:	Macmillan General Books C.S. Book Service By Post PO Box 29, Douglas I-O-M IM99 1BQ
or phone:	01624 675137, quoting title, author and credit card number.
or fax:	01624 670923, quoting title, author, and credit card number.
or Internet:	http://www.bookpost.co.uk

Please enclose a remittance* to the value of the cover price plus 75 pence per book for post and packing. Overseas customers please allow £1.00 per copy for post and packing.

*Payment may be made in sterling by UK personal cheque, Eurocheque, postal order, sterling draft or international money order, made payable to Book Service By Post.

Alternatively by Access/Visa/MasterCard

Card No. ☐☐☐☐☐☐☐☐☐☐☐☐☐☐☐☐

Expiry Date ☐☐☐☐☐☐☐☐☐☐☐☐☐☐☐☐

Signature ______________________________

Applicable only in the UK and BFPO addresses.

While every effort is made to keep prices low, it is sometimes necessary to increase prices at short notice. Pan Books reserve the right to show on covers and charge new retail prices which may differ from those advertised in the text or elsewhere.

NAME AND ADDRESS IN BLOCK CAPITAL LETTERS PLEASE

Name ______________________________

Address ______________________________

____

____

____

8/95

Please allow 28 days for delivery.
Please tick box if you do not wish to receive any additional information. ☐